D0393206

HBR Guide to
Office Politics

Harvard Business Review Guides

Arm yourself with the advice you need to succeed on the job, from the most trusted brand in business. Packed with how-to essentials from leading experts, the HBR Guides provide smart answers to your most pressing work challenges.

The titles include:

HBR Guide to Better Business Writing

HBR Guide to Coaching Employees

HBR Guide to Finance Basics for Managers

HBR Guide to Getting the Mentoring You Need

HBR Guide to Getting the Right Job

HBR Guide to Getting the Right Work Done

HBR Guide to Giving Effective Feedback

HBR Guide to Leading Teams

HBR Guide to Making Every Meeting Matter

HBR Guide to Managing Stress at Work

HBR Guide to Managing Up and Across

HBR Guide to Negotiating

HBR Guide to Networking

HBR Guide to Office Politics

HBR Guide to Persuasive Presentations

HBR Guide to Project Management

HBR Guide to
Office Politics

Karen Dillon

HARVARD BUSINESS REVIEW PRESS

Boston, Massachusetts

HBR Press Quantity Sales Discounts

Harvard Business Review Press titles are available at significant quantity discounts when purchased in bulk for client gifts, sales promotions, and premiums. Special editions, including books with corporate logos, customized covers, and letters from the company or CEO printed in the front matter, as well as excerpts of existing books, can also be created in large quantities for special needs.

For details and discount information for both print and ebook formats, contact booksales@harvardbusiness.org, tel. 800-988-0886, or www.hbr.org/bulksales.

Copyright 2015 Harvard Business School Publishing Corporation

All rights reserved

Printed in the United States of America

10 9 8 7 6 5 4 3 2 1

No part of this publication may be reproduced, stored in or introduced into a retrieval system, or transmitted, in any form, or by any means (electronic, mechanical, photocopying, recording, or otherwise), without the prior permission of the publisher. Requests for permission should be directed to permissions@hbsp.harvard.edu, or mailed to Permissions, Harvard Business School Publishing, 60 Harvard Way, Boston, Massachusetts 02163.

The web addresses referenced in this book were live and correct at the time of the book's publication but may be subject to change.

Library of Congress Cataloging-in-Publication Data

Dillon, Karen (Editor)
  HBR guide to office politics / Karen Dillon.
    pages cm. — (Harvard business review guides)
    ISBN 978-1-62527-532-5 (alk. paper)
1. Office politics.   I. Harvard business review.   II. Title.
  HF5386.5.D55 2014
  650.1'3—dc23

                                        2014023044

eISBN: 978-1-62527-534-9

The paper used in this publication meets the requirements of the American National Standard for Permanence of Paper for Publications and Documents in Libraries and Archives Z39.48-1992.

What You'll Learn

Every organization has its share of political drama: Personalities clash. Agendas compete. Turf wars erupt. It can make you crazy if you're trying to keep your head down and get your job done.

The problem is, you can't just keep your head down. You need to work productively with your colleagues—even the challenging ones—for the good of your organization and your career.

How can you do that without crossing over to the dark side? By acknowledging that power dynamics and unwritten rules exist—and by constructively navigating them. "Politics" needn't be a dirty word. You can succeed at work without being a power grabber or a corporate climber, and the expert advice in this guide will help.

You'll get better at:

- Building relationships with difficult people

- Gaining allies and influencing others

- Working through tough—but productive—conversations

- Wrangling the resources you need

- Moving up without ruffling feathers

- Dealing with the boss's pet

- Coping with office bullies and cliques

- Claiming credit when it's due

- Avoiding power games and petty rivalries

- Collaborating with competitive peers

Contents

Contents

Contents

Introduction

Every office is political.

For years, I naively thought I worked at a place that wasn't. I saw our office as more or less fair, more or less healthy, and highly inclusive—perhaps overly so—in decision making. People competed with *themselves,* I'd proudly tell prospective recruits, not with one another. And I meant it.

All those good things I believed? They were true—but only to a point, I realize with hindsight. We competed with ourselves, but also with one another. Our bosses had favorites, and we noticed. We grumbled about promotions that didn't seem deserved, assignments that didn't seem fair. People subtly found ways to elbow one another out of pole position for C-suite attention. Our office was political. Of course it was.

In a 2011 survey by the UK-based management-consulting firm Revelation, 95% of respondents said that manipulation and hidden agendas in the workplace had affected them personally. So you're in good company if these issues make you crazy. Maybe you're plagued by an office bully who constantly questions what you're doing and undermines you in meetings. Or a boss who pits you against your peers. Or a clique that wields an inordinate amount of organizational power. Perhaps you've even encountered backstabbing, one-upmanship, or shifting alliances.

You can't escape politics—no matter what your role or function. That's what Franke James, founder of Office Politics.com, has learned from the professionals around the world sharing their struggles on her website. It's inevitable even if you're self-employed. "If you're dealing with clients," James says, "you're dealing with their office politics, too. You have to make them look good. You have to understand the dynamics behind the scenes for them."

Does that mean you have to fight fire with fire? Connive and scheme? Get your blows in faster? No. As the experts and consultants cited in this guide argue, you can weather—and even participate in—politics without selling your soul. They base this observation on research, their work with clients, and abundant personal experience. And it's supported by the many examples (real but disguised) I've included throughout.

So what's the solution? It's about being *constructively* political—understanding personal dynamics among colleagues, working together for mutual advantage, and ultimately focusing on the good of the enterprise.

What happens if you simply do what's asked of you and mutter about colleagues who curry favor? Executive coach Beth Weissenberger, cofounder of the Handel Group, says you're doing yourself in. She's seen it happen again and again in her years of coaching: Those who try to stay completely out of the political fray are less likely to meet their job and career goals than those who engage. So she advises her clients to stop getting worked up about the unfairness of it all and build their own positive relationships with colleagues who will help them do their jobs well.

Ron Ashkenas, a managing partner at Schaffer Consulting, agrees. As he puts it: "It's easy to use politics as an excuse for a lack of achievement or an outlet for your frustration. But it's a lot more effective to use politics as a way to get things done." This guide will help you do that. It's not realistic to assert that you can make all of your work relationships warm and fuzzy. Let's face it, there are people you'll work with who are just jerks and no amount of advice can change that. But not having a strategy for dealing with them can definitely make things worse. And you can control much more than you might assume. Here are some common themes you'll notice throughout:

- **Question your reaction:** When people appear to be playing political games, we often think we know their motives, but sometimes we're off the mark. Step back and reevaluate: What else could be driving the behavior? Maybe it's not as vengeful as it seems—or even intentional.

- **Try removing yourself from the equation:** Everybody brings her own quirks, worries, and stresses to work. What you assume is a personal attack may have absolutely nothing to do with you.

- **Accept that not all conflict is bad:** Great performance can come out of being challenged by an aggressive colleague or being forced to collaborate with someone who you can't stand. We can and often do rise to challenges. Don't assume "uncomfortable" means bad.

- **Take charge of your fate:** Even if the playing field isn't level, you'll accomplish little by complaining about it. Assume responsibility for your progress. Don't give your manager and others any reason to dismiss you as a whiner.

- **Keep your cool:** Office bullies and other game players win every time they see they've rattled you. Never give them that satisfaction—you'll just perpetuate the problem. Stay composed, and they'll lose their power.

When asked to write this guide, I jumped at the chance. Since I understood the challenges people faced, I'd approach it with empathy. But secretly, I also felt a little smug—I thought I'd successfully navigated most political scenarios in my career. Then, after interviewing about 20 experts and synthesizing their advice on the various dilemmas, I recognized several mistakes I'd made over the years: stewing over injustices, fighting the wrong battles, making things personal when they didn't need to be. Now, looking back at those moments, I wish I'd done my research sooner.

It's never too late to learn, though—thank goodness for that.

So what's the main takeaway, if I had to boil it down to one? As organizational development and HR expert

Susan Heathfield puts it, don't try to be the boss's pet—be *everyone's* pet. That is, devote your energy to being a terrific employee and colleague. You'll find that you're less preoccupied with all the jockeying that's going on around you—and more focused on positive pursuits like performance, growth, and fulfillment.

Section 1
Political Challenges with Your Boss

Chapter 1
The Boss Who Holds You Back

The Problem

You've been quietly showing your boss the ropes for a long time. He relies on you heavily for help with everything from interpreting monthly reports to sizing up market demand to placating cranky stakeholders. Yet only his name appears on the e-mails that update higher-ups on your projects. You feel like the stagehand behind the curtain—you're running the show, but he's the one out front, taking a prolonged bow.

Why It Happens

When the person who should be your organizational guide and cheerleader keeps your smart contributions under wraps, of course you don't feel valued. Even if he's not intentionally undermining you or holding you back, it's hard to stay motivated—after all, you know your efforts will go unrecognized.

Some bosses simply don't like sharing the spotlight. Others get nervous when their shortcomings are thrown into sharp relief by a direct report's strengths. You may run into this problem with a boss who is new to his job, for example, and feels threatened by your deep organizational knowledge and close internal ties. Or perhaps your manager inherited you in a merger or a reorg and has discovered that you bring critical new skills to his team— skills everyone assumed he already had.

What to Do About It

You may fantasize about changing jobs, but you probably won't have to resort to that. You can improve your day-to-day relationship with your manager—but you'll need to lead the transformation.

Own the problem

Jessica Pryce-Jones, CEO of the UK-based leadership consultancy iOpener and author of *Happiness at Work,* says people are often too quick to dub a work relationship a failure before taking their share of responsibility for fixing it.

How can you do your part? Remember that your boss wants to succeed in his job as much as you do in yours. That will help you adopt a constructive mind-set so that you can move beyond your frustration and improve the dynamic. Think about what you share with your boss rather than what divides you: If you have only "transactional" conversations, Pryce-Jones says, you're unlikely to warm to each other. But looking for personal similarities will make it easier for you to connect professionally. Did you grow up in the same area? Do you admire the same people?

Finding common ground will help you interpret events and interactions more positively. Are there reasonable

---

BRANCHING OUT: ALEXY'S STORY

WHAT HAPPENED:
I had a "dive-bomb" manager. He'd disappear for weeks with very little contact, until he got wind of some project I was involved in. Then he would swoop in and demand reports, details, every scrap of information he could get. These urgent requests came in the form of rat-a-tat e-mails arriving at 10 PM or later. Often he'd take my responses to board meetings, passing off the work as his own. Then he'd lecture me on the need to keep him in the loop.

WHAT I DID:
I tried to keep my boss informed, but he'd ignore my updates and still somehow be taken by surprise. So I found myself pointing him to e-mails or memos I'd sent weeks earlier, which just annoyed him. I started to feel cut off from the rest of the organization, so I reached out to managers above him, asking if I could help with their cross-functional initiatives. That way, when he came back and demanded to know what was going on, I could say, "So-and-so signed off," and he'd have to drop it. I also began to let people know what ideas and contributions were mine because he was taking credit for everything. I copied key people on my e-mail updates to him, spoke up more in meetings, made casual comments that showed my depth of knowledge, and attached my name to documents I created for him.

DID ALEXY GET IT RIGHT?
It's hard to strike a healthy balance with an alternately indifferent and needy boss who shuts you off from others. Alexy was smart to put his name on his contributions and form alliances with other senior managers—otherwise, he'd have remained isolated and resentful—but it probably wasn't the best idea to go behind his paranoid boss's back (or over his head). That just fed the perception that he couldn't be trusted with independence and visibility.

---

explanations for what you perceive as negative signals? Maybe your boss appears to be shutting you out of critical meetings with his boss, for instance—but it's really because one-on-ones feel more efficient to him, not because he wants to keep you from growing and advancing.

Once you're open to his point of view, you can begin treating him as you'd like to be treated: Find genuine opportunities to make him look good. "Tell someone he respects—perhaps one of his peers—about an insight he shared with you or something he accomplished that you admired," Pryce-Jones suggests. And express your appreciation after he helps you meet an important goal or solve a tough problem. You don't need to be effusive. Just sincerely acknowledge what he's done for you. At the very least, you'll lower his defenses. Best case, you'll set a gracious example that he wants to follow.

Tap his former direct reports

If you can easily get in touch with someone who used to work for your boss, invite her out for coffee. (You may already know someone who managed the relationship effectively if you've been in the organization for a while. Otherwise, you might need to rely on friends to discreetly point you in the right direction.) Explain that you're eager to develop in your role and that you'd like to pick her brain about her experience working with and learning from your boss. Pitch it as a tutorial for you, not as a gripe session: See if she can share insights about his mentoring style, for example, and tips on how to earn his trust so that he'll feel comfortable giving you stretch assignments and placing you on cross-functional teams. Even if you feel safe confiding in this person, assume that anything you say could make its way back to your boss and edit yourself accordingly.

If the former report has only bad news for you—your boss really *is* a jerk—at least you're forewarned. You know it's not personal to you and that someone else understands what you're going through if you need a sympathetic ear.

Katie, a research scientist (names and details are disguised in examples throughout this guide), suffered for several years under a supervisor who treated her with contempt. Katie had been recruited into her plum position by her boss's boss, so she assumed that her boss resented her for that reason. Not wanting to make waves, she kept quiet and tried to do a good job. But then a chance conversation with one of his former direct reports led her to realize that the guy didn't hate *her*—he was generally a bad manager and grumpy guy. That gave Katie the courage to stand up to him in one-on-one meetings. "It was so helpful to realize that it wasn't just me," Katie recalls. "I stopped taking it personally and started thinking about how to get him to back off instead."

Network with his peers

Make sure your manager's peers know how hard you work and how much you care about the company. If your boss isn't giving you opportunities to demonstrate that to others, you'll need to do it by slowly building your own relationships with people in a position of influence, says INSEAD leadership professor Herminia Ibarra. Start by getting to know a couple of people outside your immediate group (see chapter 16, "Forging Alliances"). The relationships can be casual—based initially on chitchat about movies or hobbies—or you can ask for formal introductions. Do a six-degrees-of-separation exercise if you can't think of an easy way to connect: Who in my circle can introduce me to this person?

One ally isn't enough, even if it's someone with lots of power. No matter how well placed that person is, your boss can damage your reputation with others in the company if you've got no one else in the senior ranks looking out for you.

Paula learned this the hard way. She emerged from a massive corporate reshuffle with her job intact and a new manager, Liz. Though Liz needed her expertise to get up and running, things between them quickly got rocky since Paula clearly had the CEO's ear. When the CEO asked Paula to handle a project for him on her own, Liz went into attack mode—criticizing her in public meetings, finding fault with her data. Paula saw the CEO's support as guaranteed job security, so she continued to work around Liz at his behest. But over time, Liz chipped away at her reputation—and the CEO's confidence in Paula eroded. She was eventually fired from the company.

Had Paula forged ties with a few influential people a level or two up, says leadership consultant Ron Ashkenas, she would have been less vulnerable to Liz's steady campaign against her.

Confront him

If you haven't managed to subtly change the dynamic with your boss, it might be time to speak openly with him about the problem. It's a risky move, but it could be your last, best chance to fix the situation, says Ashkenas. Don't have this conversation if you aren't prepared to switch jobs; it could backfire if your boss really does have it in for you. But in a case like that, you wouldn't want to stick around anyway.

Approach your boss in the most constructive way possible. Let him know that *you're on his side.* Say you want to find better ways to support him. No good will come of sulking with your arms folded or ranting about how unappreciated you are. Even if that's true, your boss won't respond calmly to that—he'll get defensive.

After you've set a positive tone by putting his needs front and center, make it clear that you're looking to grow, too. Explain that you're hoping to do that within the organization—ideally with his guidance. But say you'll also consider outside opportunities after a certain amount of time has passed (offer a reasonable time frame—maybe a year). To give him something concrete to work with, describe your big-picture professional goals and how you envision getting there. Suppose, for instance, you're eager to build your analytical skills: Volunteer to take on assignments that will require you to gather and interpret data. For example, you might comb through customer renewal rates to see if there are any patterns worth discussing. Ask your boss if he has other suggestions for developing those skills in your current role or if he'd recommend ways to get other senior managers in the company to see you in a new, high-potential light.

Of course, once your cards are on the table, be prepared for things not to go your way. But at least you'll have given yourself and your boss every opportunity to right the course.

Chapter 2
The Boss Who Pits You Against Your Colleagues

The Problem

Your boss has you competing against your peers for her respect and attention. It's a "reindeer games" scenario—only one of you can win some coveted prize, whether it's the chance to lead a team, get a promotion, or just have a moment in the limelight. She has created a horrible, cutthroat environment for an otherwise collegial group of direct reports.

Why It Happens

Though some bosses don't realize they're creating this problem, in many cases it's a deliberate management tactic: Task several people with solving a business challenge, and make it an implicit horse race. Even when a

RETALIATION: ANDREA'S STORY

WHAT HAPPENED:

I worked in a small organization where two of us had the same title but very different jobs in practice. Our boss didn't see a problem with the ambiguity, but it created tension. I managed a team of people. My peer didn't manage anyone, but she had significant influence. She took every opportunity to undermine me by bad-mouthing me to my team. My direct reports would defend me, but it was rattling for them. In many cases, they'd come to me to tell me what was happening.

WHAT I DID:

I told my boss, and he said, "Don't worry, I'll take care of it." I assumed he spoke to her, because for two or three months, the behavior disappeared. But then she began sending around nasty e-mails about me—sometimes "inadvertently" copying me. Here's the really bad part: I figured out that people like that can be manipulated because they're convinced that others are actively working against them. So it was easy to fight back. I'd say things like, "I saw the owner of the company today, and we had a really good chat." That would freak her out. It implied that I was having some kind of exclusive conversation with the big boss. I wasn't—but she didn't know that. Ultimately her behavior got out of control, and she unspooled publicly. She got fired around the same time I left the company.

DID ANDREA GET IT RIGHT?

Andrea was effective, but at great cost to her colleague and herself. She allowed herself to slip down to her colleague's level—and it didn't make her any happier, just guiltier. She would have felt better taking a higher road, calling her colleague on the bad behavior and asking her boss to create more-distinct job titles and descriptions to clarify their responsibilities.

promotion isn't on the table, senior executives often leave roles and responsibilities ambiguous as a test. They want to see who can take the pressure, who will rise to the occasion, who wants to get ahead badly enough to throw some sharp elbows.

Abraham Lincoln famously assembled a "team of rivals." He harnessed their competitive energy to bring out the best in each member and to produce the greatest results as a group. Bosses do the same. In some industries, such as investment banking and consulting, it's even considered a rite of passage, observes leadership consultant Jessica Pryce-Jones. The boss thinks, "I made *my* way to the top through healthy competition, so why shouldn't you?"

What to Do About It

An environment like this is frustrating for both you and your peers—and it can actually harm performance. When people focus intensely on beating one another out, they inevitably lose sight of larger goals and the greater good. Here are some ways to establish a friendlier, more collaborative dynamic—even when your boss (knowingly or not) sets the stage for conflict.

Make a pact

You and your colleagues can find your own ways of working together that don't ratchet up the competition. Leadership consultant Kathryn Heath figured this out early in her career, when an indifferent boss unwittingly set up a rivalry between Heath and a coworker. "We were in two different areas," Heath recalls, "but we needed to work together. Our boss didn't make roles and decision rights clear for us, so we had to sort them out ourselves." The colleague wanted to take the lead, just tapping Heath for whatever support he needed. But Heath didn't intend to play a supporting role. In fact, her colleague relied on resources *she* controlled.

Rather than engage in passive-aggressive games, Heath decided to have a straightforward discussion with him about how they could work together on a level field. "It was a tough conversation," she recalls, "because we were held accountable for different things." They tried to keep emotion out of it by focusing on coming to an understanding that would benefit both of their teams. "We came up with a detailed plan for how we'd handle certain situations. And we agreed to not make any big commitments or moves without talking to each other first." It wasn't a perfect solution, but by dealing with the issue directly, they diffused what could have been an incendiary relationship.

Establish ground rules, advises Susan Heathfield, an organizational development and HR expert. What if your colleague is playing dirty—by one-upping you in meetings, for example, or leaving you out of the loop so that you'll look clueless? Describe exactly what you see him doing, and ask him to stop. You may not feel comfortable confronting him, but work up the courage to do it. He'll be more likely to play fair in the future because he probably doesn't enjoy confrontation any more than you do. "He usually gets away with his behavior," says Heathfield, "so it's key to call him on it. If you allow it to continue unchecked, that trains him to do it more often—or to more of an extreme."

Call a time-out

You don't have to duke it out just because your boss has thrown you and a colleague in the ring. You can refuse to fight. Mary Davis Holt, one of Heath's partners, learned this in a past job—but not as soon as she'd have liked. Her boss had put her on a project with someone without making clear assignments, and it created conflict. Though Holt and her colleague had sat down in the beginning to sort out who would do what, over time she realized that she had allowed herself to do 80% of the work while her colleague was happy to claim credit for leading the effort.

"I probably should have recognized the imbalance earlier," she says. "But I was so eager for the next promotion, I wanted to show my willingness to go with the flow and be a flexible team player." The more she put up with, the more she saw her colleague as an adversary. In hindsight, what does she wish she'd done? Though she's glad she didn't let her anger erupt into a nasty fight over division of labor, she says, "I should have asked my boss to clarify our respective responsibilities right away." Once she spoke up and her boss realized what he'd set in motion, he agreed to step in to better divide the tasks.

Manage up

Tell your boss how you feel about the situation, but be diplomatic and constructive. If she thinks you're grousing, she won't take your concerns seriously. Or she might conclude that you have difficulty getting along with others (see chapter 4, "The Boss's Pet"). Discuss it with your colleague first, advises Heathfield—and then meet with your boss, perhaps together. Say you'd both like to stop vying for the spotlight because it's distracting you from doing your best work. Ask if she can avoid putting you in competitive situations (and give a few examples, in case she's not tuned in to the competition) so that you can both be more productive—to the benefit of all.

Some bosses think fostering internal competition helps them identify the truly talented, "like some kind of Darwinian gauntlet," says Pryce-Jones. She recently advised a junior investment banker who faced that problem. His boss tried to pit him directly against another colleague: Whoever had recommended the best-performing investments by the end of six months would be the "winner." The prize? The boss's favor—and job security. So the fledgling banker approached his boss with a different idea: Could he and his colleague work *together* to come up with the best picks? He identified reasons that would be better for the company, citing research about the benefits of collaboration. The boss agreed to try the experiment, and he's been pleased with the results. In Pryce-Jones's experience, this example isn't an outlier. "Most bosses are open to trying a different tack," she says. "Especially when you say, 'Here's how you could get more out of me.'"

Chapter 3
The Control-Freak Boss

The Problem

Your boss is smothering you. At first you thought, "It's because I'm new—that's why he insists on reviewing every document before I distribute it and sitting in on all my meetings." But now that you're no longer learning your role, the tight leash feels downright oppressive and embarrassing. The other day, he actually scolded you for having a hallway chat with one of his peers about an idea you've been kicking around. You're hardworking, competent, smart. How are you ever going to escape your boss's shadow?

Why It Happens

Your boss is acting this way for a reason—though he may not be aware of it. Think about what could be driving his behavior. Try to get past the easy answer—it's probably not that he's evil or that he truly wants to keep you from being successful. Rather, his actions might be explained by factors that have little to do with you, such as a poor understanding of his role as manager, a micromanaging boss of his own, a lack of motivation to question how he's always done things, or personal insecurity.

What to Do About It

"Few people get the guidance they need to become good managers," says Carol Walker, a principal at Prepared to Lead, "and just about all of them have some insecurities about their competence. Accepting this may help you feel a little less frustrated with your boss. It's likely he's simply a flawed human being who thinks he is doing his best."

It can be hard to see things that way when your boss isn't cutting *you* any slack. His harping about every small misstep you take can feel overwhelmingly personal. But you don't have to resign yourself to being nitpicked to death. "You can't change your boss," Walker says, "but you have more power to improve the situation than you probably realize. It must be a process, not an event. It's a process that *you* have to own and direct."

Avoid his panic buttons

Form an educated guess about where your boss's sensitivities lie. If you believe, for example, that he's intimidated by those above him, think of ways you can alleviate that pressure, such as running reports to better prepare him for meetings with his manager. Or perhaps he's afraid that people don't perceive him as essential, and he's on a tear to prove how much you and others need him. Dispel his fears, advises communication and branding expert Dorie Clark, author of *Reinventing You*. Show him that you value his guidance. Ask him for feedback. Bring him any news you hear, and take your ideas to him before sharing them with others. As your boss begins to trust that you'll come to him without prompting, he may loosen his grip.

Once you get to know him better, you'll gain more insight into the areas he's touchy about. Looking at what has set him off historically—budget surprises? schedule changes?—will help you find ways of putting him at ease now, says Clark. Then you can assemble a dashboard to keep your boss as informed as he wants to be. Agree on your top priorities and the metrics that will demonstrate progress, and ask him how often he'd like to receive updates.

Your proactive, tailored-to-him system will comfort him. That's important, since micromanaging often stems from a boss's insecurity. "I call it 'snoopervising,'" says Stewart Tubbs, former dean of the College of Business at Eastern Michigan University. Turn the behavior around by preempting it: Tell your boss you want him to feel he can count on you and your work. Frequently report to him on your progress—before he can even think to check up on you. And use language that signals active listening. Tubbs recalls one young man who said "Consider it done" at the end of every meeting with his boss. Another young woman said "Understood" to show that she was engaged and on board. This isn't about simply placating your boss, notes Tubbs. You have to earn his trust by performing well. These employees consistently delivered, so over time their verbal reassurance meant something and helped their bosses relax.

Don't fight it

If you openly rebel against micromanagement, Clark cautions, your boss may clamp down even more. Leadership consultant Ron Ashkenas agrees. Instead of viewing it as a blow to your ego, he suggests, think about how you might actually benefit from it. Your boss may have your best interests in mind. Perhaps he wants to ensure that you have a sound understanding of the company's protocol or the most effective ways to work the system to get things done.

Regardless of the cause, says Ashkenas, accept that your boss may have something important to teach you. Just try to learn as much as you can, as quickly as you can—in case he doesn't eventually let up and you decide you can't take it anymore.

Scrutinize yourself

If your boss doesn't appear to have faith in your ability to do your job, consider whether you've given him a reason to feel this way. Have you missed important deadlines? Delivered presentations that fell flat? Assembled proposals that failed to win business? Take a hard look at yourself—and look around. If your boss isn't micromanaging other colleagues, his behavior could be a clue that you're underperforming.

If you suspect that's the case, ask him about it, says Clark. Tell him you feel he's monitoring you extra closely and you want to understand what's behind it. Is there a particular area where he feels you need guidance? Some bosses are reluctant to be straight with employees about their shortcomings, especially if criticism might be met with hostility. They may go to extremes, such as overly aggressive monitoring, to avoid having awkward conversations. So make it easier for your boss: Say you're genuinely interested in feedback on your weaknesses, even if it's hard to hear. Stay calm as you listen to the feedback (don't even let a grimace cross your face). Once you get a clear sense of where you stand, you'll have a better shot at addressing his concerns.

Thank your boss for his insights and tell him that you want to come back to him with an improvement plan. You might need to soothe your ego for a day or two, but the sooner you return to him with a proposal, the more seriously he'll take you. Ask if he can recommend potential mentors (inside or outside the company). See if human resources might help by suggesting a course to develop your project management or public speaking skills. If you approach the conversation openly—and then earnestly work on your shortcomings—you'll likely find your boss trusting you more and more.

Look ahead

Focusing on your future may help you and your boss interact more productively in the present. So initiate a discussion about your long-term professional goals. Set up a one-on-one meeting, or ask if you can use one of your scheduled check-ins to talk about your role. Explain that you want to start communicating more regularly—and explicitly—about your growth and about how else you

MICROMANAGED: LUKE'S STORY

WHAT HAPPENED:

After I'd worked for years at a large company, my two bosses moved me to a small division to run the problem child: a start-up that had already cycled through three directors in two years. My bosses had many other people reporting to them, but I was their chief focus because the new venture had already burned through a lot of money on an untested model. They micro-managed like crazy. They had no idea what would work, so they tried 10 new things a week, yanking the team this way and that. I realized pretty quickly that my job was to manage them, to serve as a heat shield in hopes of keeping my staff on something re-sembling a plan.

But I wasn't able to do that at our staff lunches at the end of each week, when everyone in the division piled into a large conference room to share updates and brainstorm ideas. The room was filled with both senior and junior staff. Anything could set off my more volatile boss, whose sidekick would then join him in publicly stomping me or my managers to a pulp over a perceived lapse in procedure or strategy. When the controller couldn't spit out numbers fast enough to answer any and all questions fired at him—what do we know about X this week?— he was pummeled, and then so was I for not having him pre-pare properly for the meeting. And on it went, week after week. I would spend each weekend scrambling to contain whatever damage had been done or rushing off to the next fire that the bosses had declared our New Top Priority. These lunches were, of course, in addition to daily floggings, plus phone calls night and day (Sunday, 7 AM: "Why didn't you know this server was down since 4 AM?").

WHAT I DID:

Finally, after two years of this, my beleaguered controller and I hit upon one number that hadn't yet been questioned: How much had we spent on these lunches? When I mentioned the number in a cost-cutting discussion, suddenly the lunches went from weekly to biweekly. Then monthly. Then not at all. I didn't cure my bosses of their management styles. But at least I man-aged to take some of the sting out of my week.

DID LUKE GET IT RIGHT?

Luke probably couldn't have diffused his bosses' control-freak tendencies altogether in such a highly charged situation—the running of a troubled start-up division. But he was savvy in using costs, an issue they cared about deeply, to get them to drop the painful, unproductive lunches. Luke could have also tried to get ahead of their expectations. Knowing they saw such meetings as opportunities to grill employees on the spot, Luke could have used the time to showcase how his staff was on top of problems. And he could have met with his boss privately in advance to suss out areas of concern and then prepared his staff to address them with metrics or analysis. Finally, he could have proposed cost-control measures on a monthly or quarterly basis, because he knew his bosses would always respond favorably to that sort of discussion.

could support the department. Give him some examples of the types of projects you'd like to work on and the future role you envision for yourself. Say you're ready for more independence, and you'd like some opportunities to demonstrate that. Emphasize how important his feedback is to your growth. Offer some ideas on how you might realize your vision—and see if he can suggest others.

Keep the conversation constructive and forward-looking. Complaining about the past won't open your boss's mind or make him want to support you, Walker says. Being positive and taking ownership will. Let him know that you appreciate his guidance, but you're eager to spread your wings a little, too.

Ashkenas says junior colleagues at his firm have had this conversation with him—and it's worked well. He admits he struggles to fight his own micromanager tendencies. "I don't think I'm a control freak, but I do have strong feelings about quality," he says. His colleagues were subtle, but he understood what they were getting at ("Ron, do you still want to see the final slides and documents in advance?" "Would it be all right if I worked directly with the client to finish these?"). When people have diplomatically pointed this out to him, he's been happy to find ways to step back—once they've demonstrated that they can meet his quality standards.

Ease your boss's fears by emphasizing that you're willing to take this in steps. Chances are he'll welcome your enthusiastic, respectful approach—not resist it. If he does resist, there's little point in fighting, Ashkenas says. "If your boss isn't ready or willing to let go, it might take more time for him to trust you and have confidence." You can revisit the subject down the line. Or, Ashkenas says, it might be possible that his need for being involved is so deep-seated and emotional that it will never change.

If your boss is receptive, however, thank him. But that meeting is just the beginning. Offer to update him on your progress at your regular check-ins, advises Walker. Use those meetings to share your thinking with him— not just what you're going to do but *why*. Ultimately your boss has to trust not only that you'll follow his instructions but also that you'll tackle problems in a way he approves. Close each meeting by proposing next steps and getting his buy-in.

Develop other champions

If your boss is micromanaging you, others may notice and start questioning your skills. That's why it's critical to build relationships outside his ken. "It's so important not to have all your eggs in one basket. Have points of contact with other people who can see your good work," says leadership expert Herminia Ibarra. You want them to get to know you and see what you're capable of when you're unfettered by your controlling boss.

Join interdepartmental committees, and get involved in cross-disciplinary pursuits. Organize a companywide volunteer day or a brown-bag lunch series that brings industry luminaries into your office. But avoid dabbling in areas where your boss considers himself the expert: He might feel upstaged by your efforts and pull the plug on them—or try to insinuate himself. Tell him what you'd like to do *before* you volunteer so that you don't take him by surprise and trigger his instinct to micromanage.

Chapter 4
The Boss's Pet

The Problem

Your boss has a pet employee who gets the most inter-esting assignments and special perks, such as flextime and an expense account. She invites her pet to social events, confides inappropriately to him about "prob-lem" colleagues, and acts like they're old friends. And she doesn't seem to hold him to the same standards that apply to the rest of your team: You all log in extra hours and go above and beyond, while he appears to just coast along. It drives you crazy.

Why It Happens

Sometimes favoritism is actually fair: The pet has a burn-ing talent and desire to excel, works hard without com-plaining, and shares the boss's goals and vision. Under-standably, the boss is high on her star performer.

But what if she favors an average performer? In that case, her pet is just a buddy. Like everyone else, your boss enjoys having friends at work. So she may latch on to an employee she sees as a kindred spirit—someone with whom she's comfortable. Or perhaps she's inherited a direct report she's already friends with outside of work.

BEST IN SHOW: ALICE'S STORY

WHAT HAPPENED:
When I started my first job as a journalist at a magazine in New York, I swiftly realized that my boss—the maker or breaker of careers there—favored people with the "right" pedigree. He was far more impressed by someone with an Ivy League degree and Park Avenue parents than by a summa cum laude who'd put herself through a state school. For the first few months, I gnashed my teeth as I watched one of my peers—I'll call him Yale boy— get assignments and opportunities that were clearly above our entry-level position. The boss just treated Yale boy differently.

WHAT I DID:
After spending weeks complaining to my roommate about how unfair it was, I realized something: My boss didn't really know me yet. He didn't know what I was capable of doing. So of course he initially favored the guy with the same credentials he had—at that point, there was little else for him to go on. But over time, I established my skills and ambition. I threw myself into my job. I volunteered for assignments I knew I'd learn from rather than waiting for my boss to hand me growth opportunities. I also worked at building my internal network. One Sunday afternoon, my boss called the office, and I happened to be there, picking up some files. When I answered the phone, he was clearly pleased that I was working that hard. He said, "That's how people get ahead in this company." And that was true. I was promoted pretty soon after that—and Yale boy didn't stick around long enough to achieve the same.

DID ALICE GET IT RIGHT?
Once Alice stopped obsessing about her peer and started focusing on what she could control—her own development and performance—things fell into place for her. She proved to her boss that she had the skills and dedication he was looking for, and the pet's pedigree ceased to get in her way.

"Buddy" pets often take advantage of their status to obtain benefits for themselves. For example, they might ask for extra vacation days, off the record. Or they might turn a casual lunch or drinks after work into an opportunity to gain an insider's perspective, pressing for details about meetings above their pay grade and asking what the boss thinks of others in the group.

When your boss plays along, it can really stick in your craw—but don't let it.

What to Do About It

Build your own positive relationship with your boss instead of looking for ways to dethrone the pet. That's how you'll get the resources and attention you want without picking—and losing—a fight.

Stop obsessing

There's little point to moaning that your boss has a favorite and it's not fair. That's not going to change the situation. In fact, it could make things worse. "You'll just look like you're whining," says leadership consultant Jill Flynn. Both your boss and your colleagues may see it as evidence that you have trouble getting along with others (see chapter 2, "The Boss Who Pits You Against Your Colleagues"). Your boss may not want to assign you to projects with her pet for fear that you won't play nicely. And the pet might pick up your negative vibe and steer clear of you—effectively making you a pariah.

Get to know your boss

It's not sucking up to ask your boss how her weekend went or to compare notes on restaurants you'd like to try.

As Kent Lineback, coauthor of *Being the Boss*, points out, your relationship with your boss is as much a reflection of what you put into it as what your boss does, so invest time in getting to know her. Ask about the article she's writing. Invite her to coffee or lunch, without an agenda.

As a manager, I liked it when someone on my team suggested going out for lunch just to chat. Even when I was too busy to accept, I always appreciated the invitation. Bosses enjoy sharing stories about their families and vacations as much as anyone else. So cut your boss some slack and reach out to her. You may not replace her "pet," but you'll create goodwill.

Of course, even if your relationship with your boss becomes friendlier, she's still your boss. If you try to get too chummy, she may see you as a sycophant. Colleagues may think you're angling to be the new pet and start gossiping.

Communication and branding expert Dorie Clark says not to lose sight of decorum—especially when connecting through social media. If you (or your friends) post with abandon on Facebook, think twice about "friending" your boss. You can follow her on Twitter (or suggest that she follow you, if you're a prolific tweeter) as long as you keep it professional: Comment on news stories and industry trends, share useful articles recommended by members of your network, that kind of thing. This may help your boss realize that you've made smart contacts and you're in tune with important ideas.

Shine your own light

Many people are reluctant to draw attention to their successes, leadership consultant Kathryn Heath points out.

"They don't talk about their accomplishments in the first person. They say 'the team did this' instead of 'I led the team doing this.'"

Does this sound like you? If so, Heath advises getting over your modesty if you don't want the pet to consume all your boss's attention: "You can speak diplomatically, but make your contributions clear." Your busy manager may be so focused on his own challenges that he fails to notice all the good work you do. So you'll have to toot your horn a little. "Give others credit where it's due," Heath says, "but take your own credit, too."

When Heath recently reviewed a presentation that a coaching client was planning to make to her boss, she noted that the woman used "team" language to describe work she had done to win a big assignment from a new customer. Heath pointed it out, and her client revised the presentation, saying she had cultivated the customer relationship and identified the right people to help win the job. Instead of allowing her contribution to be swallowed up by a faceless team-player credit, "she told a very compelling story and got promoted."

Women tend to find this particularly difficult, Heath says, based on hundreds of 360-degree reviews that she and her colleagues have conducted. They want their performance to speak for itself. If I do good work, they think, it will be noticed—people will consider me for great assignments because I'm so productive and reliable.

Unfortunately, that's not how it works. If you want to be top of mind, you need to boost your visibility. When you attend a conference, for example, send your boss a list of 10 takeaways you'd like to share with the team when you return. You'll impress her with your initiative and team focus. And schedule a regular check-in with your boss to discuss your priorities and the progress you've made on them. At annual review time, provide a summary of your year, highlighting key accomplishments, before your boss does her write-up. This will make it easy for her to remember what you did a few months ago, too, not just your recent achievements. The meetings and documentation will serve as reminders that her pet isn't her only valuable contributor.

It's possible to make a positive impression on your boss without irritating your colleagues or behaving in a way that doesn't feel authentic to you, says organizational development and HR expert Susan Heathfield. Transform yourself into an indispensable employee. Ask for more challenging assignments. Raise your hand for projects that others don't want to do. Don't just alert your boss to problems she'll need to solve; suggest solutions. Be a team builder—tap the strengths of your coworkers, praise them when they make good contributions, elevate the discourse of the entire organization. "So often bosses are subjected to complaints," says Heathfield. "If you rise above the nonsense, that's a really good place to be."

There's a standout employee in Heathfield's own company who voluntarily mentors junior staff members, organizes social functions, and gives people in other departments a hand when she can—for instance, by helping HR screen candidates in early-stage interviews. She's approachable, knowledgeable, and trustworthy. "She's just a go-to person," Heathfield observes. "She never comes across as self-promotional. She's always focused on what would be best for *the company*." That's why no one begrudges her success or wants to see her fall from grace. It's also why she's been promoted twice in recent years—and she's on senior managers' high-potential list.

Chapter 5
The Disaffected Boss

The Problem

Your boss has "checked out." He's there physically but not in spirit. He doesn't meet regularly with your group or bother to fill any of you in on the critical decisions that senior management is wrestling with. So you're often the last ones to hear about big initiatives and changes. He doesn't fight for resources, raises, or promotions for your team—or seem to care about his people at all. If he's given up on his career, fine, but he's essentially giving up on yours, too. He's practically invisible in the organization, and you're at a loss for how to get anyone to notice your contributions so that you can advance.

Why It Happens

Some bosses become so consumed with lining up the Next Big Thing on their impressive rise to the top that they lose interest in their present roles. Others disengage as managers when they sense that their *own* futures are limited. Feeling embittered toward their companies, they may passive-aggressively refuse to manage and view that as payback for all the wrongs they've endured. They stop jockeying for budget dollars, perk allocations, new-hire slots, and so on—and quietly allow performance to fizzle out as a result.

It's also common for a boss to start phoning it in near the end of his career. People burn out over time, especially in high-pressure roles. If that's the case with your manager, he may no longer have the energy to care—and he's probably just biding his time until he can leave to focus on his photography and gardening.

Whatever the reason, it's probably not about you. It's all about him.

What to Do About It

When your boss lacks drive and commitment, it can be hard to see the upside. But you may actually benefit from his disinterest. It gives you a chance to fill the void with your own good work. If he doesn't seem to care about much of anything, then he's not likely to mind if you find ways to step in and raise your own profile, as long as your efforts don't make more work for him. Of course, you're probably on your own to figure out *what* to do. Here are some guidelines.

Try speaking up

Sometimes bosses just need a little prompting, says Boston University management professor Kathy Kram. "I've

STEPPING UP: JOHN'S STORY

WHAT HAPPENED:

In hindsight, I think I was hired because my boss had already checked out. He'd been in charge of a key division of a small private company for nearly two decades. I later learned that he'd asked the owner for equity and been denied. But the owner trusted and valued him, and my boss knew his job was safe. Essentially, he brought me in to do his job—or to make his job as easy as possible. I was hired as a number two. My boss, it soon became clear, didn't work the same hours as the rest of us. He'd blame traffic patterns for coming in midmorning. And he'd spend a lot of days "working from home." I didn't really mind, for the most part. It made my job easy and fun. He stayed out of my way, and I ran the division.

WHAT I DID:

I just tried to make him look good whenever possible, knowing it would give the owner confidence that things were being run smoothly and make my boss trust me.

We happily bumped along like that for a few years, until the owner of the company decided to sell. Then my boss kicked back into gear. I think he wanted to impress prospective owners and possibly get that equity stake he'd longed for. Suddenly he became deeply involved and dithered over every decision. He second-guessed things I'd done for years that hadn't bothered him before. I ended up feeling like I couldn't quite get it right anymore with him. When the company was sold, he didn't manage to impress the new ownership team. He resigned shortly thereafter. I stayed on long enough to find a decent new job, but I ultimately chose to leave, too.

DID JOHN GET IT RIGHT?

John was in a tough position, but he made the most of it. In some ways, he'd been given a dream job: He was the acting boss, without the bottom-line responsibility. He could learn, experiment, and develop without anyone breathing down his neck. But working for a disaffected boss isn't really a long-term career strategy. Even if the company hadn't changed hands, something else would have put an end to this unspoken agreement. His boss might have retired, or John may have decided he wanted the responsibility after all, not just the freedom.

seen managers and employees in my class who say, 'I just wish my boss would meet with me more often, give me more feedback . . .' I always pose the question 'Have you *asked* for that?' Very often, they haven't." Many bosses are oblivious to their employees' needs, Kram points out, but respond well to reasonable, diplomatic requests, especially if they're easy to grant.

Make delegation attractive

Volunteer to take on tasks your disengaged boss doesn't enjoy, suggests Stewart Tubbs, former dean of the College of Business at Eastern Michigan University. You don't want him to take offense or resent your ambition and energy—so how do you gently encourage him to delegate to you? Invite him to coffee or lunch, says Tubbs, and ask if you can do anything to lighten his workload, even on a trial basis. Say you're eager to learn new skills. Frame it as a win-win—you want to help him out and grow in the process. Most bosses would welcome the opportunity to delegate to a *willing* taker, says Tubbs, especially if you promise to send completed projects or reports to him first so that he can decide with whom and how to share them.

Fill in the gaps

Show your boss that cultivating your talents will give the team more muscle—with little or no extra effort on his part. Offer to learn new technologies, for example, or to do first drafts of reports he's responsible for. Have a good relationship with Manny in finance? Work with him to file the team's expense reports so that your boss won't have to. Sharpen the skills you know that he lacks; he might see it as a lifeboat.

Tubbs knew a young woman who got on her indifferent boss's good side by creating outstanding PowerPoint presentations. Before long, he was asking for her help with all his slides, and eventually he invited her to do some of the presenting. Once other leaders in the company saw her skills in action, they started tapping her for presentations, too. When the company later went through a severe downsizing, she was one of the few people who still had a job, primarily because her boss had come to rely on her so much. The same principle can apply to spreadsheets, social media, and so on. You may need to offer your assistance several times before the timing is right, Tubbs advises. But sooner or later, your boss will be so busy, he'll accept your offer. Do your best work when he asks you to step into the breach—you'll increase your chances of scoring repeat opportunities.

Build your own network

You probably already realize how critical it is to build relationships with colleagues, since your boss isn't doing that on behalf of your team. But he may actually be a good source of inspiration when you're deciding which people to add to your network and how to reach out to them.

Here's what communication and branding expert Dorie Clark suggests: "You might say something like 'Look, I'm really committed to the company, really interested in expanding my knowledge and working my way toward a senior role in the marketing department. But I need some guidance on networking to make that happen.

What advice would you give me?'" Your boss may surprise you with helpful ideas. Few people are so emotionally disengaged that they won't respond to a flattering request like this. "But don't just wait for the pearls of wisdom to drop," Clark adds. "Ask specific questions: 'If I want to develop strengths in X, which people do I need to talk to?' 'Who in the company really excels in that area?'"

Your boss may not go to bat for his team on a day-to-day basis, but if you engage him in a big-picture conversation about your development, he may be inclined to share contacts or ideas. It's a low-effort way for him to give you meaningful help. Ask if he'll introduce you to people he's named or if he'll keep an eye out for opportunities where you could gain more related experience, now that he knows your long-term plans.

Even if your boss can't quite muster the motivation to make introductions, you'll at least come away with a name or two. You can then create your own opportunities to meet or work with those people by volunteering for committees they work on, for example, and taking time to chat with them at lunch. Sometimes personal ties that start in cafeteria lines evolve into supportive professional relationships.

As you're working on those internal relationships, you'll want to cultivate external ones, too. Research shows that creating connections beyond your company is critical to building a robust network, says leadership expert Herminia Ibarra. That's because they exponentially increase your awareness of job opportunities in other organizations and industries, your chances of being recruited, and your ability to find mentors and allies with whom you can safely discuss career hopes and challenges. Ask colleagues if they know people outside work with expertise or knowledge you're trying to acquire—and if they do, don't be afraid to ask for introductions.

Section 2
Political Challenges with Your Colleagues

Chapter 6
The Hypercompetitive Peer

The Problem

There's one in every office: a colleague who is so competitive, so obnoxious, that she stops at nothing to get every advantage over her peers. She brags about her successes, races to be first in line for high-profile projects, weasels out of grunt work, and consistently "forgets" to mention anyone else's contributions when she's praised for something that's really a team effort. She's dead set on getting ahead, even at the expense of everyone else.

Why It Happens

People become overly competitive at work for two reasons (assuming they aren't just jerks, see chapter 15), says leadership and networking expert Brian Uzzi at Northwestern's Kellogg School of Management. Often they feel they have to fight for limited resources, such as promotions, raises, or travel. Or they may view you as a threat. "Maybe you have fresh ideas, or you do especially well in front of clients. You do something better than your peer does," Uzzi explains. "If the other person wasn't threatened by you, he or she wouldn't waste time competing."

What to Do About It

Rivalries can be deeply destructive to your career. You'll be unhappy in an environment where you have overtly or subtly hostile relationships. And you might signal to your superiors that you aren't leadership material if you get caught up in a cold war at work. Here's how to avoid the drama and the damage that comes with it.

Give her the benefit of the doubt

Thinking about your peer as hypercompetitive is actually part of the problem, says Diana McLain Smith, author of *The Elephant in the Room: How Relationships Make or Break the Success of Leaders and Organizations*. Smith points out that individuals behave better or worse depending on the relationship patterns they unwittingly create with one another. So, for example, if you view someone as a competitor, you'll treat her as one. And, in turn, she'll *feel* more competitive toward you. Your behavior will feed hers. This isn't to say that people don't have characteristic ways of behaving—a competitive person will naturally be so in all kinds of situations. "But relationships have the power to amplify or modify those ways of behaving," Smith says. Her advice? "Act as if" you believe the other person wants to succeed, but not necessarily at your expense. That trick of mind will stop you from doing things that could trigger or escalate an arms race, such as overreacting to a slight, one-upping her at meetings, or trying to undermine her before she undermines you.

Also consider whether you've accidentally done anything to provoke the attacks. It may seem to you that she's just launching into you out of spite, but an abundance of social-cognitive research shows that we're blind to our parts in these encounters. Ask a trusted colleague for a reality check. You may discover a trigger that you can easily avoid in the future.

Address the root of the problem

What if you find that you're not provoking the behavior? You'll need to figure out what's causing the competition, says Uzzi. By considering your peer's point of view and understanding what's behind her actions, you may be able to come up with a solution that eases the tension.

Suppose you're both associates trying to make partner at your firm. If just a few slots are open to new partners, competition is baked into the career track—your peer isn't to blame for it. In a case like that, Uzzi suggests approaching key decision makers to try to fix the problem at its root. You could talk to current partners before they've decided on the next crop of promotions, for example. Frame the conversation constructively: You've identified a problem, and you'd like to help address it. Maybe the cutthroat environment has led employees to leave your firm and join others. Point to those losses, and quantify their impact on the top or bottom line, to show how important it is to stop the bleeding. Ask if there's any flexibility in the promotion cycle: For instance, can the firm add two partners in one year and none the next to retain two superstars and give others time to develop their portfolios? If you and your rival are clearly assets to the company, decision makers should be receptive to a conversation like this. It's in their best interest, not just yours.

Call in friendly reinforcements

Still having problems? "What I've seen people do effectively is to band together with other colleagues," says leadership consultant Ron Ashkenas. "If there's one highly ambitious person annoying you and playing political games, she's probably also doing it to other people." Ashkenas advises gently approaching the competitive colleague with one or two peers (not a large gang—that would get her defenses up). Perhaps take her out for coffee. Your conversation should be friendly. Ask if she realizes she's been sending off a competitive vibe. "Be as specific as possible," Ashkenas says. "Give examples. If she takes it reasonably well, offer to speak up in the moment so that she can see when it's happening." Sometimes simply making a competitive colleague aware of how others perceive her behavior is enough to change the pattern.

Don't take the bait

If your colleague makes the competition public—in meetings or with your boss, for example—it's critical to keep calm, advises communication and branding expert Dorie Clark. "It will become clear to other people that she has some kind of agenda," Clark says. "Don't participate in the rivalry." If you do, you'll only fuel your colleague's ambition further and perhaps lower others' estimation of you. And, if you're spending emotional energy worrying about how you stack up against her, you won't have enough left to do your job well.

That's not to say you should let her batter you or your reputation—you'll just invite more of the same (see chapter 7, "The Bully"). Suppose your colleague Barb calls your work "irrelevant" in a staff meeting, says Smith: "I'd be prepared to respond—both publicly and one-on-one with Barb afterward."

At the meeting, you might ask dispassionately, "What makes you say so?" If she claims your logic is flawed and you've no solid data to back it up, calmly respond: "Perhaps you've missed the data and analysis on pages 5 and 6." And if she insists that the numbers don't support your case, you can say—again, in a controlled, even tone—"I realize that's your view, but saying something is irrelevant doesn't make it so. I'd be interested to hear what others think of the data and analysis."

And privately, here's how you might put her on notice: "Barb, it's hard for me to see how calling my work irrelevant would ever serve the team or even you. If anything, it makes you look bad. What was that all about?" She might surprise you with a contrite response—or she might refuse to acknowledge her behavior. Either way, you've established that you're not an easy target and that attacking you probably isn't worth her effort.

DOUBLE-CROSSED: JANET'S STORY

WHAT HAPPENED:

I'd been given the top position in my group at a relatively young age—I wasn't even 30, and my peers in other divisions were all in their 40s. So I brought in a highly ambitious number two to shore up areas where I didn't have as much expertise. On paper, Matt, my number two, looked like a better fit for certain aspects of my job, but I knew my boss trusted me and wanted me in the position. About a year in, I thought I'd built a great relationship with Matt. I'd given him lots of freedom, responsibility, and visibility, and I'd learned a lot from watching and working with him. But then a senior executive pulled me aside to tell me that Matt had gone to the top boss and asked for my job. I was flabbergasted and hurt. In hindsight, I realized that my letting him shine had allowed him to take sole credit for things and position himself as the real power player in the department.

WHAT I DID:

I called Matt into my office, closed the door (rare at our company), and told him I knew. After he stammered through an explanation that he was just expressing his ambition, I voiced my disappointment: I'd prided myself on helping him grow, and I certainly never intended to hold him back—but now he'd lost my trust. He left my office with his head hanging. I knew his ambitions wouldn't diminish, but from that point on, I didn't let him take the spotlight nearly as much. I made presentations without him. Held meetings without him. Treated him more like a direct report than a partner. Not surprisingly, he soon left the company for a prominent position in a start-up.

DID JANET GET IT RIGHT?

Tough call. Janet's decision to hire an openly ambitious number two had the potential to backfire. Janet was, in some ways, an ideal boss for Matt—it made sense to add his strengths to the bench and give him lots of room to grow. But she also had a hand in creating the problem. Self-conscious that she didn't have some of his particular expertise, she stepped *too* far out of the picture, allowing him to elbow his way past her. She looked weak, not like a confident boss who was delegating. And she should have had an open conversation with Matt early on about his ambitions and helped him chart a career path. That way, he would have viewed her as a catalyst rather than an obstacle.

Charm and disarm

If you sense that your competitive colleague feels threatened by you, find ways to support her. Say, for example, you're an academic with a gift for teaching, and your peer struggles in the classroom but does superb research. Suggest teaming up so that you can work together toward earning tenure. "Tell your colleague you'd like his or her input on your course materials," Uzzi suggests. "Or offer to have him sit in on one of your classes to provide feedback. You'll both benefit from a fresh eye and new ideas. Involving your peer in your work turns a rival into a collaborator. And a shared activity can build trust." By initiating some give-and-take, you can neutralize the perceived threat and, over time, transform the relationship into one of mutual respect.

Advocate for yourself

You can obsess about how horrible a competitor is—or you can focus on your own work and advancement. "In our firm," says executive coach Beth Weissenberger, "we see so many clients who get passed over for great jobs because their strategy was effectively 'I do a good job. Everyone should know that. My work will speak for itself.' But you're not going to be promoted if you keep your head down and steam about how unfair things are."

Weissenberger coached two high potentials who had this problem. Both had been flagged by their company as potential CFOs, but neither had articulated their career goals to their boss. So they risked losing out on chances to develop skills and gain visibility—those would go to people who spoke up and said they were looking for growth. "People need to know that you're ambitious," says Weissenberger, "as long as you don't express it in an obnoxious way. Does your boss even realize you want to be promoted? Everyone always assumes yes, but it's not always the case. You have to be very clear: 'I'm committed to doing this job well, but here's what I'm striving for. If you're looking for a future CFO candidate, I'd like to work toward the opportunity.'"

Chapter 7
The Bully

The Problem

*Your colleague is a bully. When you're speaking
in meetings, he doodles, sends e-mails, whispers to
colleagues—to the point of distracting others, and
sometimes even you, from what you're trying to say.
He's also blown up at you in front of others for petty
reasons. You dread interacting with him and find
yourself constantly waiting for his next attack. You
can't just brush it off, and it's ruining your focus at
work. The specifics may sound silly to someone who's
not experiencing this, but to you it feels like psychologi-
cal harassment.*

Why It Happens

Bullying in the workplace is not much different from
what happens on the playground. Bullies of all ages want
to manipulate the political and social power in their environment to control others. You'd think we'd outgrow it,

but it's all too common in the office: In a 2010 Workplace Bullying Institute survey conducted by Zogby International, 35% of Americans reported being bullied at work. Why is the problem so widespread? People and organizations put up with the bad behavior, afraid to confront or penalize the culprits.

What to Do About It

Being bullied at work can wreak havoc on your mental and emotional health—and your performance on the job. This happens a lot, according to a study by Christine Pearson at the Thunderbird School of Global Management and Christine Porath at Georgetown University's McDonough School of Business: 78% of participants who believed they'd been treated rudely by colleagues said they felt a decreased commitment to their work, with a direct negative effect on their performance. You—and your work—don't have to suffer. These steps will help you change the dynamic.

Consider his intentions

Some bullies don't mean to be bullies. So make sure you aren't projecting a motive that isn't there. If, for example, a peer consistently criticizes you in public, think about what he might actually be trying to accomplish, suggests leadership consultant Ron Ashkenas. Is it possible he has honorable intentions? Is he being critical of *you* or just striving to ensure high quality?

Gut-check your feelings with a work friend, or discreetly ask a trusted colleague to sit in on a meeting where the problem usually arises. A neutral perspective may help you see that the bully is not out to get you. Perhaps he's insecure in a new role and overcompensating, for instance, or he lacks the emotional intelligence to see how cutting his words and actions are. If he doesn't realize how he's coming across, you can pull him aside and ask him if everything is OK. "You seemed angry about that report. Is there something we should talk about?" As with many of the political challenges in this guide, it's entirely possible that your colleague is so wrapped up in his own thoughts or anxieties that he has no idea how he behaves toward you. Simply mentioning it might make him more self-aware.

With third-party feedback, you may also realize it's not you; it's him. Knowing that, you can shrug off his bad behavior more easily. Bullies notoriously pick on people who appear weak and fragile. Show that you're not afraid of criticism and that you're willing to stand up for yourself, and your bully may well back down.

Offer an olive branch

Disarm your bully by expressing your desire to have a good relationship with him. If he's intentionally pushing you around, he's assuming you're his adversary. So show him that you want to be on the same team. If he routinely derails your project launches, approach him before the next one: Tell him how important his input is and that you appreciate his eye for potential obstacles. After you've set a constructive example, he may change his tune: "Maybe I should have come to you with my concerns *before* the last launch . . ." Even a small concession like that can be a first step toward a more productive working relationship, says communication and branding expert Dorie Clark.

Find safety in numbers

Although you don't want to create a rival gang to counter the office bully, there is power in people banding together to support one another publicly. If you notice your bully targeting others, too, tell them about the behavior you've observed and what you've experienced yourself. Discuss how you might join forces. You could agree to stand up for one another in moments of confrontation, for instance, or help one another anticipate and address the bully's criticisms. At the very least, you'll have others to turn to when you're feeling the need to vent.

Break the pattern

It's easy to get trapped in a negative pattern with a bully. He always does certain things, and you always respond in a certain way. Maybe you find yourself complaining to a colleague after every showdown. Or you try to outbully him by doing your own masterful doodles and rolling *your* eyes when *he* talks.

How do you put an end to this destructive dance? The easiest thing to change is your own behavior. Take a quick walk outside after a frustrating encounter. Or send a positive e-mail, such as a thank-you note or a compliment to another colleague you've been meaning to write. Break the cycle of negativity with something positive.

Call him on it

Book a one-on-one meeting with the bully. Public confrontation will only exacerbate his natural tendencies, so find a space where there's no audience. Bullies often bank on the fact that people won't call them on their behavior, so your initiating a meeting will get his attention.

Suppose your bully is passive-aggressive. He makes snide remarks under his breath, and you've heard from reliable sources that he's bad-mouthing your ideas to the rest of the team. Tell him you'd like to talk to him because you get the sense he's unhappy with the proposed process changes (or whatever he's grumbling about). Stick with the facts. Don't attack him, as in "You always do such and such . . ." Instead, be specific and neutral, Clark advises. Say something like, "In today's meeting, you were muttering to yourself when we went over the process proposal. I wanted to discuss it because the same thing happened at last week's meeting, and I'm concerned about the way we're interacting. Can we talk about how we're working together so that we can both be more effective?" Be direct, but give him the opportunity to express his point of view (see chapter 14, "Conducting Difficult Conversations"). Ask him how he thinks his concerns can be addressed.

The same technique works well for colleagues who are more blatantly disrespectful: "You asked some great questions this morning, but your tone was pretty harsh. I'm wondering, was there a problem?" Odds are, the bully will back down immediately because he doesn't want a confrontation. Your directness will serve as a warning: You noticed his behavior, and you're willing to address it. At a minimum, observes organizational development and HR expert Susan Heathfield, it makes the bully think twice about targeting you in the future.

PUBLIC FLOGGING: JASON'S STORY

WHAT HAPPENED:

When I first began working in a well-known global consulting firm, a senior colleague asked me to prepare data slides for an important client presentation. He gave me very specific, detailed instructions on what he wanted and then left for the night. When I reviewed the task, I thought I could do the same thing a lot more efficiently. So that's what I did.

The next day, as we were presenting the material to the client, he called up my data slides. When he saw I hadn't done it the way he'd asked, he just went nuts. He embarrassed me in front of the client and my peers. He even followed me back to my desk after the presentation to continue haranguing me. It was awful. But that was typical of the way he treated me the entire time we both worked there.

WHAT I DID:

I avoided him. I did no favors for him, never volunteered to help him, just tried to fade into the background as far as he was concerned. And I secretly celebrated each time he made a mistake. It didn't make him go away, but at least I kept my distance.

DID JASON GET IT RIGHT?

Jason might have turned things around if he'd shown more empathy for his colleague. Yes, this guy was a bully, but he'd received no heads-up about the slides—and he'd felt blindsided in front of a big client.

After the blowup, what if Jason had approached him privately, explained that he hadn't meant to do an end run, and asked if they could figure out a better way to communicate to avoid the same situation in the future? That approach might have earned his colleague's respect. And if not, it would at least have put his bully on notice: Jason wouldn't just slink away after a public flogging like that. He'd speak up.

Go toe-to-toe with the bully

You don't need to simmer silently the next time your bully acts up. Peter Freeth, a director of UK-based Revelation Consulting, which specializes in high-performing cultures, advises his clients to calmly stand their ground during the attack: "He aggressively questions you? Ignore his questions. Absolutely ignore them. He whispers? He's drawing other people into his game. Stop and look directly at him. Continue only when he's quiet. When he does it again, stop and look. His behavior is disrespectful. You know it; everyone else knows it. The problem is that they're all too polite to do anything about it." You don't need to get caught up in retaliating. Simply take away his power to rattle you. He'll move on to another victim or perhaps put his energy toward something more useful.

Just say no

What if somebody more senior, such as your boss, is the one bullying you? You still have to draw a line. Otherwise, the entire relationship will take on a master-servant dynamic.

Leadership consultant Jessica Pryce-Jones describes a client who faced this problem—a very senior investment banker whose boss frequently made unreasonable demands on her. "He'd say, 'I want you in the office at 6:30 AM to look at my presentation.' Or 'I need to be able to reach you at 11:30 at night.'"

The banker was warm and helpful by nature. But she grew increasingly resentful when her boss started taking advantage of that. Pryce-Jones advised her to think about circumstances when she could reasonably say no—for instance, when preparing for an event would keep her awake at night. If a request seemed excessive by those standards, she needed to explain what she wouldn't do (by simply declining the request) and what she would do instead. Pryce-Jones encouraged her to try this out a few times and then evaluate how it felt. After declining a couple of such requests, she had a clearer sense of her boundaries—and she felt much less resentful. This gave her more energy for what she said yes to. Making active decisions empowered her and increased her confidence.

Work up the courage to say no a couple of times to make it clear that you aren't a pushover. Of course, if you worry about your job security or if your work environment becomes hostile, you should report it to human resources.

Chapter 8
The Clique

The Problem

There's a group of "golden" people in your office. They get assigned to high-profile projects, receive lots of public praise for their work, and ascend the ranks faster than others. They're a tight crowd: They have one another's backs in meetings and socialize after work. You've never been tapped to be on their teams. You're good at your job; you're just not in the right circle.

Why It Happens

Office cliques form—and thrive—for lots of reasons. Sometimes, for instance, you'll find bands of colleagues who have moved together from other companies, particularly in industries that are worlds unto themselves, such as media and technology. (And it makes sense: As leadership expert Herminia Ibarra points out, research consistently shows that the key to getting a new job is networking.) When people know one another socially or from past jobs, they naturally have stronger, deeper ties.

FITTING IN: REBECCA'S STORY

WHAT HAPPENED:

I was thrilled when I got a foot-in-the-door position at a really hot company. But I was definitely low woman on the totem pole, with a low salary to match. On days that my coworkers rounded one another up for lunch, I literally couldn't afford to join them, but I wanted them to ask me. They were the office in crowd. Not only did they eat together—they shared weekend plans and tales, and had an easy, comfortable rapport with the boss. They were never mean to me, but I was invisible to them.

WHAT I DID:

I collaborated with one of the "cool kids" on a couple of projects, as her junior, and I worked really hard on them, which made her look good. She warmed up to me after that and started extending invitations to join the group for dinner and drinks after work—usually spontaneously, so I didn't have time to budget. But I said yes the first time I was asked, not wanting to lose my opening.

After that night, they still occasionally invited me along. And occasionally not. I didn't say yes every time—didn't have the cash—but I knew I'd somehow cracked the group. And with that, I was more accepted at work. I felt more part of things, and I think my work was better, too. I gained confidence. But in time, I also realized I more naturally gravitated toward people who took joy in their work. Bonding over drinks wasn't really my thing. So I started working, somewhat voluntarily, late nights in the office. Those of us who stayed after hours got free dinner and cabs home on the company, so money wasn't an issue. The dinners I shared huddled in an office conference room felt much more like bonding experiences to me. We talked about work, we talked about ourselves, we built mutual respect. Little by little, I found my own in crowd, and it was a much better fit.

DID REBECCA GET IT RIGHT?

Rebecca found a toehold into the clique, and that was all to the good, because it helped her integrate with her colleagues. And she learned soon enough that she was better off making personal connections with colleagues she respected and admired than hanging out with the flashiest group. Building her own in crowd worked beautifully, because those relationships would make her happier and more connected with her job in the long run.

Of course, they also tend to gel if they frequently work together on projects. They understand and trust one another's strengths and weaknesses, and even have shorthand ways of communicating that outsiders might not understand at first. In other words, they cultivate a group "emotional intelligence," to use psychologist Daniel Goleman's term. In teams, emotional intelligence can be critical to doing great work, but it's not automatic—it must develop over time.

When senior managers see a group operating so smoothly, why *wouldn't* they go with that well-oiled machine for the next big project? Though they don't mean to deny others chances to excel and advance, that's often the unfortunate outcome.

What to Do About It

If you find yourself outside the right clique at work, you may miss out on opportunities—both professional and social. But you don't have to sit at your desk just waiting for someone to notice you and invite you along. Break into the group—or build your own.

Work with the existing clique

Don't let the golden children get all the heat and light. Even if you're not invited to contribute to their big projects, express interest in them. Leadership consultant Ron Ashkenas advises, "You can say to your boss or colleagues, 'I know I'm not on that assignment, but could I sit in on a status meeting to learn more about it?'" And once you're in the room, offer to pitch in. Raise your hand for *any* role to start with, says Ashkenas: "Be willing to do some scut work to prove yourself." Volunteer for all-hands-on-deck QA work, for instance, or offer to update process documentation. When you do help out, overdeliver—and look for even more ways to showcase what you can do. People will start to see what you bring to the party, and in time you may find yourself a regular in the go-to group. Ashkenas recalls a client's secretary who successfully did this years ago. "She volunteered to sit in on meetings and take notes," Ashkenas says. "She created great summaries and eventually helped do some secondary research in support of the project. A few months later, my client had promoted her to an analyst role and hired a new secretary."

Another alternative, Ashkenas says, is to ask a member of the golden group to mentor you. That will require a long-term commitment on both sides. But if you can identify someone in the clique you could learn from—and she'd be willing to invest time and energy in your development—that might provide you with entrée as well.

Form your own alliances

Maybe chumminess at the office feels artificial to you or seems like a waste of time. You may be thinking, Why put aside my "real" work just to make friends? But the reality is, it'll help you do your work more effectively.

First, you'll gain support for your ideas. No matter how respected you might be individually, you'll always bolster your case by lining up allies. Suppose, for example, you're proposing a new CRM database. You'll need buy-in from your IT colleagues because they'll be involved in picking and maintaining the software if the project becomes a reality. So you'll want a buddy in IT to help you think through how to enlist his team's support before you bring your idea to senior managers.

Second, people will share more information with you if they feel connected to you. When they catch wind of a big decision or organizational change in the offing, you'll hear about it sooner—so you'll have more time to prepare for it. If you're not part of an informal alliance, people simply won't think to clue you in.

To form alliances that'll give your ideas traction and keep you informed, you'll need to network deliberately and efficiently (see chapter 16, "Forging Alliances"). Ask your boss and a trusted mentor or two which people in the organization you should get to know better, suggest leadership consultants Kathryn Heath, Mary Davis Holt, and Jill Flynn. Set up lunches with those folks. Find out about their pet projects and challenges.

Flynn adds: "Get a big-picture view of whatever company you are working in. What are the challenges? Who are the leaders? Have that down cold in your mind." Then, she says, you can seize opportunities to talk with colleagues about these issues. But make your outreach subtle. "You shouldn't make an appointment to interview the person and just sit there taking notes," suggests Flynn. "Formal is your last resort."

Flynn coached someone who had identified a power player she wanted to learn from at her company. But he was busy and didn't know her well, and they didn't interact much on the job. So Flynn's client figured out a natural way to collaborate with him and build a relationship. She offered to help him with a big training session he held once a year—to organize it, run errands, whatever he needed. He gratefully accepted, and that was the start of a productive mentoring relationship.

Create opportunities to socialize with the colleagues you're eager to know. Another client of Flynn's discovered that a couple of important people in her company took the train home at a certain time every day. So for a few weeks, she kept an eye out for them on their way to the train. When she spotted them, she walked along with them, chatting as they went. "It worked," Flynn says. "They became comfortable with her, and she learned a lot."

It's essential to do all this in a way that feels and looks authentic—you don't want to come off as a stalker. The key is to initiate relationships *before you need them*, so it's not just about angling for favors. Otherwise, you won't have the stomach for it, and you'll end up avoiding alliances rather than building them. And that can have a devastating impact on your career, says Kent Lineback, coauthor of *Being the Boss*. Very few people rise to the top of their profession without allies to support them along the way. It might be critical, for example, to have them backing your candidacy for a sought-after promotion. Or to have a go-to team for high-profile projects you need to knock out of the park.

Lineback knows this all too well. Years ago, he didn't focus on building relationships outside his own department, even though he held a senior management position. "I just didn't *want* to," he recalls. During a strategic-review meeting, Lineback shared his ideas about what direction the company should go. He was stunned when nobody responded with even a glimmer of enthusiasm. He had carefully worked through his proposal with members of his own group, but he hadn't gut-checked or socialized it with anyone in the room ahead of time. And no one there felt obliged to give him the benefit of the doubt—he didn't have anyone in his camp. After the meeting, a consultant involved in the review pulled Lineback aside and offered his two cents on what went wrong: "You didn't build any bridges," he said.

"I knew he was right," Lineback says. "It was one of those instant recognitions. I hadn't wanted to dilute my idea, make it messy, by bringing other senior people in. Shame on me. After a while, you realize you have to be plugged in."

Connecting with colleagues doesn't have to be self-serving or manipulative. Be transparent with them about what you're hoping to achieve, whether it's gaining a broader understanding of the organization, exploring other career paths in the company, or something else entirely. But also make it clear that you want the relationships to go both ways. And then, of course, look for opportunities to support *them*.

This worked for Heath and Flynn, who formed an alliance back when they worked in different departments of the same company. Over the years, they've found ways to support each other, discovered opportunities for each other, and generally enjoyed working together. Initially Heath reported to Flynn, but they later became peers. "It's not a social relationship," Heath explains, "but we're best friends in a professional sense." While they were trying to figure out how to navigate the company, they'd each pass along feedback or news that might be helpful to the other. "We would trade information," Heath says. On more than one occasion, they trusted each other to discuss job opportunities that would take them outside the company. "One time I was getting ready to take another job and she said, 'You're running away from something . . .'" Heath recalls. "We were pretty straight with each other. You need to have a truth teller in your group, and we just became that for each other."

They ultimately parlayed their successful partnership into a consulting firm, Flynn Heath Holt Leadership (with Mary Davis Holt). If you can build strong relationships with people you respect—as they did—the time you invest will have long-term benefits for you and your allies.

Chapter 9
The Credit Stealer

The Problem

You've put in long hours on a project, and some of your best ideas made the final cut. Yet no one knows it. When your colleague presented the final proposal at a recent team meeting, she didn't specifically claim all the credit for herself. But she avoided mentioning you and used the pronoun "I" every time she could. Afterward, your boss thanked her for doing such a great job—and your colleague still said nothing about your contributions. Once or twice this kind of thing could be an honest mistake. But it happens all the time. How will you ever get ahead if no one sees the good work you do?

Why It Happens

People may appear to take credit for your work without realizing it. When they're making a presentation or talking to a superior, they genuinely get caught up in their own role and simply miss the opportunity to name other key players. And collaborative environments can make it tricky to even identify who contributed what. Most bosses don't go digging for those details because what they ultimately care about is the team's work as a whole.

What's more, in some professions, the culture makes it very difficult to get credit for your work before you reach a certain level in the hierarchy. In management consulting, for example, the senior partner on an assignment usually gets the client's accolades, whether she's done the work or just supervised at arm's length. In academia, the tenured professor almost always appears first in an article byline, although her junior team may have done most of the research. Even in the court system, hardworking, bright judicial clerks help shape the opinions of their bosses without much—if any—recognition.

But sometimes, a more insidious motive lurks behind credit stealing: The thief is insecure or desperate to look better to her superiors—and figures she can get away with it if she's stealthy, says leadership and networking expert Brian Uzzi.

What to Do About It

Don't rush to point fingers. Consider whether there's any chance you're wrong. Maybe your colleague *did* have the same idea as you, or maybe you heard it kicked around somewhere else without remembering it. Uzzi's research suggests it's common for people to overvalue their own contributions. "It's called *fundamental attribution error*," he says. "We all think that our role is much bigger than everybody else's. Ask five people, 'How much did you contribute to this project?' Every person will say he did 50% of the work." So if you think someone hijacked the credit for your hard work, make sure your perception isn't skewed. "Check with others to see if they agree," Uzzi says. Don't just assume the worst.

But if, upon reflection, you *do* see a problem, try the following steps to solve it.

Stop it before it starts

If you've been burned before on a team, prevent it from happening again by writing down the group's expectations and assignments up front, advises leadership consultant Ron Ashkenas. Begin with a discussion about goals. Then, as a group, create a work plan that supports them: Lay out all the tasks, sequence them, and agree on individuals' assignments. If you and your colleagues draft the work plan together, there will be less room for confusion later about who was responsible for what. You'll also have a written history of your shared intentions. If your work involves a presentation, don't let someone fly solo. Divide up the slides—and share the visibility.

Clear the air

If you're not able to preempt the credit stealer, have a candid conversation with her. Give specific examples. For instance: "Sophia, when you presented our report, I was a little surprised when you said, '*I* stayed up all night . . .' because we both did. Can we talk about why you said that?" Many times just pointing out the behavior will put an end to it, says communication and branding expert Dorie Clark. Your colleague may immediately apologize and say, "I didn't realize it came across that way."

Or she may simply deny the charge: "That's ridiculous—I did almost all the work on this project myself." Don't accept that answer. Push back. Showing her that you won't quietly step aside makes it harder for her to gloss over your efforts next time.

Go to your boss

It's always best if you can work things out directly with your colleague. Tattling over a minor incident or two may antagonize her and put her on the defensive. "You don't want to create an enemy just because of a mistake," Clark advises. But after you've talked to her, if she refuses to see your side of the situation and continues her behavior, go to your boss. Otherwise, your morale and motivation will suffer. When you speak with your boss, keep your tone neutral. Talk about the impact on the business, not just on you, so that you won't sound petty or overly emotional. Maybe your colleague's grandstanding has caused others to avoid collaborating with her, for example, or your team is earning a reputation in the company for being embroiled in controversy and ineffective. Review the steps you've already taken. Suggest another solution or two that you've thought of, and ask your boss for his input.

What If the Credit Stealer Is Your Boss?

Many managers believe that a direct report's success is rightfully their success, too. After all, they laid out the vision, assigned the tasks, nurtured and developed the talent, and so on. In some organizations, Uzzi says, that's simply a given.

Your boss may not even remember where she gets every idea. And she may get annoyed if you seem easily wounded by what she considers a normal by-product of collaboration.

Take a long-term view

The "reward" for your contributions may not be immediate applause but something more tangible in the future—such as better resources for your group or a promotion down the line. That's how it works at MTV. A case study of the entertainment company found that many of its best ideas, such as the wildly popular *Real World* television series, actually come from unpaid interns. But as a policy, no single person or team gets credit. It's always "MTV" as a whole, largely because the company wants to retain intellectual property rights. But MTV does, Uzzi observes, track individuals' contributions. The people who make a significant impact during their tenure get the best recommendations for paid jobs at other companies looking for talent trained in the MTV brand.

MTV evaluates interns informally through observations of teamwork and feedback from peers. If someone consistently adds to the creative process or plays a significant role in developing a product that no one could have come up with alone—such as a new concept for a show—his contributions will get noticed. Comedian and nighttime talk-show host Jon Stewart was once an MTV intern. He worked on a new idea called "being real," which became the DNA for reality TV and helped get Stewart on the short list of high potentials at MTV. MTV rewards team-based work by "basically being a big employment agency," Uzzi says, where placement in good, paying jobs after an MTV internship is the "currency used to reward people over the long run."

Even though your boss doesn't give you a nod for every accomplishment, your overall impact may not be lost on her. Does she have a track record of eventually rewarding those who've paid their dues? If so, it's probably worth being patient. If not, you may need to have a chat.

Tread very, very carefully

You can get credit without embarrassing your boss, but it's a delicate procedure. Organizational development and HR expert Susan Heathfield recalls a consulting client who did this effectively. Assigned to work on a companywide profit-improvement project, Heathfield's client ended up doing the lion's share of the research, but her boss delivered almost all the findings. That made sense because he needed to get buy-in for the ideas. But Heathfield's client wanted senior managers to know she'd played a key role. So she found ways to graciously add supporting facts and background information during meetings. She didn't upstage her boss, but she subtly demonstrated her level of knowledge and involvement with the project. "Over time," Heathfield says, "it became clear to the big bosses who really knew what was going on." The company promoted her to oversee the project full time—"with huge kudos and credit," Heathfield adds.

Of course, diplomacy is critical. Don't try to put your boss in her place in front of others. "If she takes credit for your work, there's a very good chance she's doing it out of some deep-seated personal need for recognition," says Kent Lineback, coauthor of *Being the Boss*. So she won't forgive you for a public shaming—and she'll probably retaliate. Instead, advises Lineback, talk to your boss privately. Tell her that you're motivated by recognition for your ideas. If she doesn't start sharing the credit after you've brought it up, she's not likely to change her ways. Unless you can derive longer-term rewards from your work (as in the MTV example described earlier), it might be time to look for another job.

THWARTING THE THIEF: BERNARDO'S STORY

WHAT HAPPENED:
A colleague put one of my PowerPoint slides into his own deck— without mentioning my name in a source line. He just presented my ideas as his own.

WHAT I DID:
I went to see him and said, "I feel like this is my intellectual property. If you're going to use it, I'd like credit." But he pushed back, saying that people in our organization shared everything, so there wasn't a need for a source line. We went back and forth. When he still didn't budge, I involved third parties in our network—people we both respected. He knew if his reputation for withholding credit spread, no one would want to collaborate with him. So he backed down. Not only did he stop using the slide—he stopped giving the lecture entirely. All to avoid putting a single line of credit in a 40-slide deck. To him, giving credit diminished his originality in front of his audience. But in the end, he cut himself off from the very material that could have made him appear more original—and more collaborative.

DID BERNARDO GET IT RIGHT?
Bernardo handled the situation well. He approached his colleague respectfully and asked for nothing more than a source line—hardly an unreasonable request, even in an organization that "shared everything." Had he backed down, his colleague would have taken that as tacit permission to keep plagiarizing.

Chapter 10
Managing a Disgruntled Former Peer

The Problem

A recent, and well-deserved, promotion changed the social structure in your group. A pal and former peer now reports to you—and he doesn't like it. He acts as if he doesn't realize you're the boss, bypassing you whenever possible. Sometimes he's downright hostile. It's awkward for both of you. You're afraid you'll look ineffectual if you don't get it under control quickly, but you're not sure it's possible to fix the situation and save the relationship.

Why It Happens

It's common for a former peer to resist a reporting change like this. The problem stems largely from the complex issue of self-esteem, says Carol Walker, a principal at Prepared to Lead. We all benchmark ourselves against colleagues to gauge how much we've achieved, for instance, and how much people respect us. We don't even realize we're doing it most of the time. But when our guideposts change—as they do when a peer becomes the boss—it disturbs our sense of self, Walker points out. No one likes to lose relative position.

So your promotion probably dealt a significant blow to your peer's ego: He wasn't chosen for the role, after all. And he may have less access to senior leaders than before. If your promotion created a new level of management, for example, he may now be a rung lower on the org chart, reporting to someone with a lesser title. These are very real losses—and he might act out as a result. It can be especially difficult—on both sides—if he's older than you. You may feel guilty about the promotion and hyperaware of your youth; he may be embarrassed that he was passed over for someone less seasoned. That tension makes any interaction uncomfortable at first. And if you were friends, it complicates matters even further. You may struggle to maintain personal ties as you try to establish the parameters of your new professional relationship.

What to Do About It

It's tempting to dismiss your employee's reaction as shallow, selfish, or status-driven. You may even resent it, Walker says, and vent to others about it. Ironically, he's probably venting about *your* behavior, which may be less than sterling if your self-esteem feels threatened, too.

When your former peer doesn't respect the new pecking order, it can be difficult to empathize with him. But resist the urge to act out peevishly, Walker cautions. That would amount to stamping your feet in a childish tantrum and screaming "I'm the boss now—you have to do what I say!" As a manager—especially a newly promoted one—you need to make sure your people perform well. You'll get more energy and better contributions from them by fostering healthy egos.

So what should you do when your former peer lashes out? "Recognize the behavior for what it is—a natural reaction to unwelcome change," Walker says. "Your challenge is to restore equilibrium as quickly as possible."

Reset your own expectations

After a shake-up in the org chart, can you and your former peer still grab drinks after work? Can you continue to trade snarky comments about annoying colleagues?

Yes and no, says leadership consultant Jessica Pryce-Jones. You have to acknowledge that your relationship has fundamentally changed, even if you're good friends. You can't remain an inner-circle confidante—or treat your direct report as one—now that you're the boss. But that doesn't mean that you suddenly have to defriend your pal on Facebook or scratch his name off your holiday card list. Just put a little distance between the two of you. Find a new sounding board, and encourage him to do the same.

Expect him to test you to see how much of the original friendship remains intact. Maybe he'll ask you for information that you shouldn't share, for instance, or wait until you really push before he responds to your requests. You may be tempted to cave because you feel uncomfortable about the change in chain of command. But you have to set new boundaries. If your colleague asks you an inappropriate question—"How much are you budgeting for raises this year?" or "What does the CEO think of so-and-so?" or "What happened in the executive committee meeting this morning?"—don't answer. Count to 10 before responding, if you have to. Think about whether your boss would want you to share those details, and edit yourself accordingly. You can end the conversation with a statement such as "It's not appropriate for me to say right now." If you dismiss the question quickly but firmly, he will probably stop asking. If he persists, be direct: "You know I can't share confidential management information with you. Please don't keep asking me. I promise I'll fill you in when the time is right."

Check your perspective

Before going into problem-solving mode, though, make sure there's actually a problem to solve. You might be projecting negative feelings onto your new report ("I would feel that way, so that's how he must feel").

Step back and do a reality check, advises Pryce-Jones. Do you have concrete evidence that he's upset about the situation? For example, is he avoiding you? Meeting with your boss on his own without informing you? Has anyone told you that he's specifically complained about you? If not, you may be imagining hostility that doesn't exist.

LEAPFROGGING: MICHAEL'S STORY

WHAT HAPPENED:

When I was in my late 20s, my boss created a new position for me that had me leapfrogging over two colleagues who used to be higher than I was on the org chart. They would now report to me. I was thrilled about the promotion, but I was so unprepared for it that I didn't pause to think through how to handle the situation with my colleagues. My boss told them he was promoting me and then briefly let me know that it hadn't gone too well, but that was my first and last conversation with him about it. One of them quit the next day. I felt terrible about it—I had considered us friends and didn't even have a chance to discuss it with him. But the other one, he stuck around. And that was worse than leaving, because he fought back with classic passive-aggressive behavior. We were in the middle of a huge project, and he suddenly went from putting in a great effort to doing the minimum. I kept finding mistakes in his part of the project and started panicking that he was actually putting them there on purpose.

WHAT I DID:

I did two very stupid things: First, I apologized to him for getting my promotion. And then I just worked harder. Instead of addressing any of the real issues, I decided that I personally had to make sure everything was perfect. It was exhausting, both emotionally and physically. He seemed to take pleasure in the frantic circles I was running. When the project was finished, I saw a mistake in the final report the first day it went public. I wanted to cry. When my colleague quit about a month later, I was relieved.

WHAT SHOULD MICHAEL HAVE DONE?

Michael didn't do anything right here. He was so unprepared to be the boss that he never *acted* like the boss. He didn't clear the air with his colleagues, so they had no choice but to assume (correctly) that he hadn't considered the situation from their point of view. When the first one resigned, Michael should have responded to the wake-up call by having an open, direct conversation with the remaining colleague. But by keeping mum and picking up all the slack himself, he just made it easy for that colleague to misbehave. From the beginning, Michael should have emphasized his desire for a productive relationship, clearly laid out the team's needs, and asked his direct reports how he might help them succeed in their roles.

Talk it out

If you do find evidence of bitterness, say something right away. Ideally, though, you'd ward off resentment as soon as you're promoted. In the beginning, it may be enough to show a little sensitivity and say, "I know we'll need to work through a new professional relationship. I hope we can be candid with each other about that." Delaying the conversation won't make it easier—it will only allow hard feelings to build up. Though you may be uncomfortable explicitly discussing the change in roles, you're in charge now, so it's your responsibility to take the lead.

It's not possible to have a comprehensive and constructive conversation about your new relationship the minute your promotion is announced. But briefly acknowledging that things are different now will help soothe frayed nerves and put you in a stronger position to have a positive, forward-looking conversation down the road. Assure your former peer that he's still one of your most trusted colleagues, and give him time to adjust to the new dynamic. And then, if he struggles with the transition, get that out in the open.

That's the advice leadership consultant Ron Ashkenas recently gave a client who'd been promoted to CEO over a tight-knit group of peers. One colleague in particular struggled with the new hierarchy because she'd wanted the job. Making matters worse, everybody who worked with them closely watched the tense relationship, viewing it as the new CEO's first test. "I advised him to have a private, honest conversation with his former peer," says

Ashkenas. "That's how you defuse this kind of problem: You address it head-on and focus on both parties' needs. Say that you want to be successful in your role—and you want your new report to be successful, too." Ashkenas says that approach helped repair the relationship and alleviate tension so that the former colleagues could work together productively.

If you think the dynamics are strained, say so when you sit down to talk, suggests Pryce-Jones ("This isn't easy for either of us . . ."). Assure your colleague that you'll consider previous conversations confidential, especially if you've shared personal thoughts with each other in the past. Then talk about how you look forward to strengthening your working relationship. You're striking a balance here: Clarify what you expect from the other person—but also express your loyalty and support.

Even after you've taken these steps, does your former peer seem reluctant to open up? Offer a few observations about what you think his concerns might be, and then ask him to fill in the picture for you. Make it easier to discuss taboo topics, such as visibility and status, by bringing them up yourself. Tell him how much you value him and that you're committed to helping him reach his professional goals. Say you realize it'll take a little time to earn his trust in your new role. And ask him to speak up (respectfully) when you make mistakes so that you can learn from them. That will emphasize the two-way nature of your relationship.

Todd, a newly promoted manager in a small media company, recounts facing just this situation with his former peer Carlos. They had both reported to the same senior manager, but that person decided to have Carlos report to Todd instead. While the move was initially awkward for both of them, they went to an off-site lunch to hash out their concerns. When Carlos confessed to never feeling valued by the former senior manager in the first place, it was easy for Todd to build on their existing relationship of trust. "You know that I understand your strengths as well as anybody here," he said. "Tell me what you'd like to see yourself doing that you aren't doing already."

Of course, one air-clearing conversation isn't enough, says Ashkenas. You'll continue to face issues that require candid discussion. For the CEO in Ashkenas's example, meetings presented a challenge. When he raised provocative questions to stimulate healthy debate, his former peer froze, unsure whether it was permissible to challenge her boss in public. Puzzled by her silence, the CEO asked about it later in a one-on-one, and the colleague spoke openly about her concerns. That was the only way to identify and solve the problem: The CEO explained that he saw debate as a good thing, as long as it was collegial, and that thawed the ice.

Correct course

Even if you and your employee have both behaved badly and are feeling a little hostile toward each other, you can turn things around. Leadership and networking expert Brian Uzzi suggests the following three steps, based on his extensive research and consulting work in leadership and organizational change:

1. **Redirection:** Look for ways to redirect your new report's—and your own—negative feelings. For instance, when you talk, try blaming circumstances rather than people. Set up the meeting in a conference room or an off-site spot. Calling him into your office would only reinforce that you are now in charge and he isn't. "Moreover," Uzzi says, "it shows you need to lean on the crutch of your authority. Neutral ground indicates that you have confidence in your leadership position." You might even try to find something *better* than neutral ground, Uzzi suggests, such as a place your new report likes. Meeting at his or her favorite restaurant can signal your intention to invest in the new report. "That can evoke positive feelings that spill over into the discussion," Uzzi says. As obvious as those tactics might seem, Uzzi's research shows that they *do* work. Redirection allows the person to continue feeling his natural emotions but shifts them from a destructive place to a safer one.

2. **Reciprocity:** Now that you're the boss, you'll need your new direct report to do things for you— preferably willingly. Before you ask for something, try giving him something: an unexpected perk, perhaps, or an opportunity to showcase a strength. Also, find common ground to discuss. Maybe you're both committed to the success of an R&D effort, and you share the view that the

demographic of your ideal customer is shifting. Focus on addressing that—working toward a common goal will help replace the hostility with something more productive. You might, for example, ask him to attend an important management meeting so that he can inform the discussion with his technical expertise. By doing this, you'll signal that you're looking for ways for him to grow and gain exposure to more senior managers. You'll also demonstrate that you trust him to make smart contributions. Small steps like this will help lay a more positive foundation for your relationship. "The secret to effective relationship building through reciprocity is to give before you ask," Uzzi says. "If you give and ask at the same time, you don't create a relationship—you create a transaction."

3. **Rationality:** Have a rational discussion to clarify your expectations. You can't avoid this conversation; it's critical if he is to trust that your other steps (redirection and reciprocity) aren't just ploys to marginalize him by pushing him into new assignments or areas that might be out of the mainstream workflow. "To avoid skepticism creeping back into the relationship," Uzzi says, "never leave the conversation with the other party saying to himself, 'So-and-so was great to me in the meeting. He offered me many valuable things, but he didn't say what he wanted

in return. I wonder when the other shoe will drop?'" Say what you need to, and be specific, whether it's "I need you to be my ally" or "We need to make some changes to your job description." Discussing your expectations may actually relieve stress for your new direct report. A clear sense of what you expect of him, how he fits into the big picture, and what role he'll play for the team will allay his fears about you as the new boss. And, Uzzi advises, "Don't say you need the other person in a needy way. A good approach is to let the other party know that he or she is valuable and that your offer is distinctive, but that you also have other relationship options. This elevates the offer by expressing its value (others want it, too)." One way to do that, Uzzi suggests, is to say "I wanted to give you the right of first refusal . . ."

Bring your boss into the loop

Don't just hope *your* boss won't notice any adjustment problems you and your direct report are having, advises Walker. Let her know it's been a tough transition and explain how you're approaching the situation. She may have anticipated difficulties on both sides but held off to see if you could figure out a path on your own first, to show she does consider you to be in charge now. But asking her for guidance won't make you look "green" in your new role. View it as a chance to highlight your problem-solving abilities. Describe your game plan, but let her know you'd appreciate her feedback and other suggestions. Complaining about your employee's behavior without detailing what you're doing to manage it will only lead your boss to think that you aren't taking ownership. If she offers help, don't be afraid to accept. Is your former peer continually doing end runs around you? Ask your boss to redirect him back to you when he tries to go over your head with a problem. But keep your tone even and calm: Present yourself as sensitive, patient, and on top of the situation. Raising and addressing issues in a prompt and professional manner will help your boss see your management skill.

What if your colleague still acts up after you've tried all these tips? Then it's time to wield your new legitimate authority, says Stewart Tubbs, former dean of the College of Business at Eastern Michigan University.

"I had this situation myself with a couple of people who had wanted to be dean but didn't get the job," says Tubbs. "Boy, they were not about to cooperate with me when I was appointed instead. Eventually, I had to sit them down and say 'We can do this the easy way or the hard way. The easy way is I'll support you, you'll support me, and we'll work together. The hard way? If you don't come around, we'll have to start making things formal. We'll have 30-, 60-, and 90-day performance reviews. If you continue to rebel and aren't meeting your goals, I will take up the matter with HR in formal disciplinary proceedings. All things considered, I'd like to do it the easy way.'" Eventually, both colleagues left the university, having never really come around. But Tubbs felt that he had done all he could to get the relationships back in line before resorting to dramatic measures.

Of course, you can say all this in your way—in your own voice. But if you've tried everything else to no avail, you'll probably need to pull rank to put an end to the game playing.

Section 3
Political Challenges in Your Organization

Chapter 11
Surviving the Office Outing

The Problem

*Your company has a couple of splashy employee events
every year—and that kind of "forced fun" is not your
cup of tea. You like most of your colleagues, but you
dread the thought of trust falls, or pelting one another
with paint balls, or laughing politely at your boss's
bad jokes over charred burgers and potato salad. You'd
rather skip it, but everyone is expected to attend, so
your absence would be duly noted.*

Why It Happens

Companies organize events like these with good intentions—often to raise morale, help employees blow off
steam in an informal setting, foster team building and
idea sharing, or reward people for good performance. After all, research shows time and again that engaged employees are far more likely to be loyal to an organization,

and those with friends in the workplace are both happier and more productive. But the challenge is knowing exactly how to socialize with coworkers you're *not* already close to: Whom do you talk to? What if the conversation doesn't come naturally? How can you make a good impression without feeling fake? How do you strike the right tone? How much should you let your guard down? Where do you draw the line between casual and inappropriate? These sorts of questions can stress you out and prevent you from enjoying the very benefits the event is meant to provide.

What to Do About It

You have to make a reasonable effort to participate. It's not uncommon for people to bow out, citing pressing deadlines or last-minute conflicts—and many companies don't make social events mandatory. But as communication and branding expert Dorie Clark points out, avoiding them sends a bad signal. It suggests you're disinterested in the company and your colleagues—or perhaps that you don't see a future for yourself there. Those perceptions aside, the carefully crafted excuse you make once might be greeted with skeptical smirks when you use it a second or third time.

Here are some guidelines for gracefully navigating office outings and actually getting something positive from them.

Find a comfortable way to participate

If you're lucky, you welcome the opportunity to hang out with your coworkers because you're fond of them. But even if that's not the case, says leadership coach Susan Alvey, a principal at Pemberton Coaching, assume the most positive perspective you can. "Instead of looking for the first moment to escape, think about how you can have a good time." If the outing involves something you can't imagine yourself doing, you don't have to go *all* in. You'll get extra credit with your colleagues, Clark adds, just by showing a little team spirit. If you really can't stand to play ultimate Frisbee, for example, get involved in a different way. Go and cheer on your teammates. Bring lemonade to the barbecue afterward. Take photos. But show up.

Focus on connecting

View the outing as a personal-growth exercise, Clark advises: "Use it to hone one of the most talked about, but least practiced, skills in corporate life: asking questions that draw people out and then really *listening* to their answers." Before your event, think about what you could ask your colleagues—even boring Floyd from HQ—that would help you relate to them. "It's a low-stakes laboratory," Clark says. If you can figure out how to engage with Floyd, you can also learn to have richer conversations with clients or collaborators.

Beth Weissenberger, an executive coach, agrees: "I ask my clients before they go to an event, 'How many people will you meet?'" Give yourself a concrete, obtainable goal. For example, you might plan to have conversations with five colleagues you don't know well—or make a point of speaking to the CEO for the first time.

Part of connecting is letting more people know who *you* are. This doesn't mean you need to chat up everyone in your path or prattle on about your accomplishments. "When people are nervous, they either retreat or talk incessantly about themselves," observes Boston University management professor Kathy Kram. A better way to make your presence felt is to demonstrate your sincere interest in others. "As you encounter people," she says, "really focus on building the relationship. Express genuine curiosity instead of worrying about being impressive. Listen, and then share your thoughts in response to what you're hearing." And if you're shy, don't torture yourself to overperform. "It's not necessary to stay to the bitter end," advises Kram. Just meet your goal and gracefully excuse yourself. You don't have to make a big deal of leaving—try a simple "I've enjoyed talking with you. I'm going to head out now, but I look forward to learning more about your project next time I see you." No one is taking attendance at the end of the party. A trip to the bathroom could take a discreet left turn to the coatroom and out the door.

Don't check your inhibitions at the door

Of course, as you're trying to relax and be yourself, you'll want to maintain some sense of decorum. We're all adults—and most of us know our limits—yet we've all seen people have too many drinks at office events. Yes, an extra glass of wine might ease your frazzled nerves or help you endure sitting next to the world's most pedantic colleague, but be more disciplined with your intake than you would with close friends. People aren't likely to notice what you're drinking, but they'll certainly notice if you start acting goofy or making indiscreet comments. And they'll remember serious missteps for a long time.

If you mess up, own up

So what if you wake up the morning after and realize that you may have crossed the line at the office party? "If you do something embarrassing, own up to it," Alvey says. You don't need to send out a mass e-mail to everyone in the company. But have the courage to apologize to anyone who witnessed your behavior.

If it happened in front of a group, touch base with each person individually. Don't belabor it—self-flagellation isn't required. Alvey recommends a short, direct statement along these lines: "I realize that my behavior might have put you in a difficult position, and I never meant to do that." Or try a little bit of humor, company culture permitting: "No more punch for me!"

Admit the mistake, apologize, and move on. "Psychologically, it might seem easier to slink around and try to avoid people," Clark says, "but ultimately, that's not the right thing." *You* become the elephant in the room. People might whisper when you walk in, or you'll catch them staring at you or laughing. It may or may not be about you, but your imagination will run wild. Much better to put the elephant away by taking control of the apology. That way, at least, smirks, eye rolls, or looks of pity can't catch you off guard. You'll have already owned up.

Make amends face-to-face if you can. But if you feel that e-mail is your best option (perhaps because it's the only way you can manage to get the words out), omit the embarrassing particulars—written messages stick around and may be forwarded.

If your mistake was a big one, apologies might not be enough. Weissenberger recently worked with a media company that fired a new employee in his first week because he got drunk at an event and ended up making out with a subordinate.

"Once you mess up your reputation, it's hard to get it back," Weissenberger says. "Not impossible, but hard."

Chapter 12
Lasting Through Layoffs

The Problem

Something big is happening in the senior ranks at your company, and it can't be good. You've noticed lots of closed-door meetings and heard rumors of layoffs. Everyone you know feels vulnerable. You've seen colleagues chatting up muckety-mucks and taking them out to lunch, but that feels calculated and phony to you. You want to keep your job—and ideally take on more responsibility if there's an opportunity—but not by glad-handing the leadership team. How can you protect your career without sacrificing your self-respect?

Why It Happens

Even strong companies go through reorgs, for a host of reasons: CEOs face constant pressure to do more with less. New leaders want to put their mark on the firms they run. Organizations rework their business models to stay competitive in evolving industries. When times are changing, even the most stable, reliable departments can be seen as obstacles to progress.

As much as we'd like our leaders to include us in any thinking about pending layoffs, they have to keep the information closely held. It's probably painful for them to have those closed-door meetings—they know they're about to make life-altering decisions. But the last thing they need is for panic to set in while they're sorting out the specifics. There's still work to be done. A company can't lose its day-to-day momentum. And legal and security considerations may make it impossible to share information more widely the organization can't risk having employees take valuable data, contacts, or intellectual property out of the building when they get wind they're going to lose their jobs. When layoffs do come, the news must be announced on a very tight schedule to control who knows what, and when, no matter how much compassion a well-intended manager may want to show his employees.

What to Do About It

When forces beyond your control threaten to reshape your organization, don't just passively await your fate. Create a survival strategy. You'll have a far better chance of sticking around and maybe even improving your position. This isn't about playing games or backstabbing others—it's about managing how decision makers perceive you and the value you bring.

Keep calm and carry on

It's easy to imagine all kinds of things happening behind those closed doors. But you might be wrong. Or maybe you're right to suspect a reorg, but there's still plenty of time for names to change on a layoff list. Either way, it does no good to fly into a panic. Act like a survivor, not a victim. That's what *Harvard Business Review* authors Janet Banks and Diane Coutu say in "How to Protect Your Job in a Recession" (September 2008), and it's good advice no matter what the economic climate. You don't have to be stoic or turn into a corporate cheerleader. But maintain your composure and professional demeanor—demonstrate your ability to focus and keep up your good work, despite swirling uncertainty. If you stop going full throttle because you might be out the door tomorrow, you're not doing yourself any favors: You may land yourself a spot on the layoff list if one does exist.

So rise above whatever back-channel chatter may be consuming your colleagues, says leadership consultant Jessica Pryce-Jones. People who spend a lot of time whispering aren't proving themselves indispensable. It's natural that the topic of pending layoffs will come up, especially when the boss is out of earshot. And there's always someone in the group who excels at sniffing out gossip and wants to share tidbits. But don't indulge in those discussions—walk away from the coffee machine if the conversation devolves. Quickly get meetings back on track when people start griping instead of working. Be a leader, even if you aren't officially one.

If you need to talk through your fears, turn to a trusted friend or relative. "Don't air your concerns with colleagues or in a way that your boss might hear," cautions one manager who has led teams through corporate restructurings several times in her career. That goes double for venting on Facebook or Twitter: It can only harm your chances of surviving if colleagues or managers see you as a complainer or, worse, a confidentiality risk.

That said, you'll need to keep up your network connections in a time of job uncertainty, says communication and branding expert Dorie Clark—and social media will help you do that. She notes that LinkedIn activity can signal when layoffs are brewing: You'll suddenly see lots of people in an organization updating their profiles and adding new connections. Get ahead of the LinkedIn rush, advises Clark. Refreshing your profile early on will allow your contacts to receive your skills and experience updates before hasty detail changes and requests to connect come through en masse from panicked peers. You can also start putting out feelers for informational interviews and job leads by touching base with former colleagues and superconnectors in your network. Often when people are laid off, they're given just a few minutes to clean out their desks—and they're not allowed to take any information, including contacts, from their computers. So make sure your LinkedIn connections are current and active long before you get called to HR for an unscheduled meeting. Also, tweet about industry trends you're noticing, smart articles you're reading—anything to show your contacts that you're still engaged in your work.

Mentally prepare

If you're bracing yourself for layoffs, much of your stress comes from losing control. Big decisions that will affect your future are out of your hands. Though you probably can't prevent a reorg if one is in the works, you can get ready to weather one—which will help alleviate some of your anxiety.

Start by visualizing scenarios: What will you do if you lose your job? How about if you keep your job, but you end up on a team of one, doing work that was previously handled by six people? And so on. Develop a Plan B, C, and D, with strategies ranging from seeking a new position in the company to signing up with different head-hunters to taking a sabbatical to consider what you'd like to do next. In practical terms, it's always wise to keep your résumé up to date. But if you haven't done that, give it a fresh look and see if you can jazz it up with new experiences, skills, and responsibilities.

Also, assess your rainy day fund—how long can you afford to be out of work? (Clearly, it's not the best time to make a down payment on a new house or sign a lease that requires stretching your salary.) If you don't have much of a cushion to fall back on, map out your expenses and see where you can start saving. All this helps you reclaim some control, which puts you in a more constructive frame of mind. You'll be less inclined to engage in politically risky behavior, such as kvetching with colleagues, making bitter remarks to your manager, or openly surfing the internet and looking for jobs instead of doing your work.

And try to get a sense of how long the reorg process will take, says Pryce-Jones, so that you'll know how far you'll have to stretch your resilience. If you have a good relationship with your boss, ask about the time frame for pending decisions, or discreetly tap your broader internal network for clues.

Get ahead of your boss's questions

Downsizing is often about streamlining operations. In large-scale restructurings, for example, companies typically focus on producing more and spending less, not on cutting specific individuals loose. With this in mind, Pryce-Jones advises, try to suss out your boss's concerns—and help address them.

If you feel comfortable approaching your boss directly, do so, and present yourself as a problem solver. She might not be at liberty to let you in on specifics, but she may still welcome a proactive conversation. You could open with something like, "I realize you probably can't share details at this point, but I'm guessing you've had to consider how we might do things more efficiently. If you'd like, I can share some ideas in a brief proposal. Am I jumping the gun, or would that be helpful?" Tell her you've been thinking through how the team can shave time off a complicated process, for example, or handle more tasks. Arm her with solutions to recommend to decision makers.

Position yourself

Don't assume your manager and others above her already know how valuable you are. Show them, says leadership coach Susan Alvey. Write up your contributions to the company, and sit down with your boss to review them—even if the potential for layoffs isn't out in the open. Your boss will certainly figure out that you've picked up the vibe, but there's no reason to wait to put your best foot forward, as long as you don't appear desperate or pushy. You're indicating that you know she has difficult decisions to make and you want to make your best case to stay. Give her an updated résumé or just a list of bullets. But clearly spell out how you've added to the organization's success. This makes it easy for her to forward your document or copy and paste from it as she formulates her plan. If she's agonizing over which names to put on a layoff list, she may be grateful for reasons to keep you aboard.

Of course, don't suggest other candidates for that list. Your boss probably knows where the dead wood is, and your pointing it out will signal that you aren't a team player. This also isn't the time to say how underappreciated you are or how much a layoff would hurt you ("I'm the primary breadwinner in our family"). That's the last thing she wants to hear if she's struggling with a tough layoff decision—and it can actually make you more vulnerable by giving you a pathetic aura. Rather, Alvey says, emphasize the positive: Remind your boss of projects and accomplishments that demonstrate your breadth and depth of skill and your ability to adapt.

Your goal is to make a strong case for why you deserve a spot on the new, streamlined team. Quantify the value you add to the company, suggests Clark. If, for example, you bring in revenue that offsets big costs, pull together a simple spreadsheet that highlights this. If it's hard to calculate your impact in dollars—perhaps you're a communications specialist, for example—find ways that you *can* keep score. Track the number of media hits you get for your company and how much your company's Twitter following has increased since you've been leading its social media efforts. Do you work in an operational role? Document productivity improvements you've made. You

---

REINVENTION: HANNAH'S STORY

WHAT HAPPENED:
Where I work, a major restructuring brought two previously battling divisions together. My boss and the other unit head became comanagers of the combined group, so neither division "won" over the other. But as they began to articulate a vision for the newly formed unit, I could see that my role would soon become outdated.

WHAT I DID:
I polished up my résumé, highlighting skills that I knew would be useful in the new structure, and shared it with my managers. And I asked lots of questions about changes to our strategy and business model to show that I cared about where we were headed as a group. Essentially, I reintroduced myself to my managers and proposed changing my role to better support their evolving goals. I was genuinely enthused about the possibilities I'd identified, which I think showed.

DID HANNAH GET IT RIGHT?
By clarifying what her role could become—and showing that she had the skills and experience to pull it off—Hannah secured a place for herself and for several of her direct reports in the new order. Though she didn't know for sure whether she'd have a job after the dust settled, she acted in a way that said "I'm with you," which signaled strength, flexibility, and loyalty. She figured out how she and her team could help her managers implement their strategic plans instead of waiting for them to sort everything out.

don't have to cite *every* achievement. Hit the highlights, and be ready to continue or deepen the discussion if your boss requests it.

Still feeling uneasy after reviewing your skills and contributions with your boss? You may want to discuss alternatives to layoffs. Say you've learned that your organization is cutting a certain amount from its budget. Would you volunteer to go half-time to keep your job? Could you suggest job sharing? "It's a risky strategy," Alvey says, because you might give something up without needing to. But you may be able to have an honest conversation in the abstract: "Would it make a difference if some people went part time?" Talk about possibilities without necessarily offering yourself up as a sacrificial lamb. If you enlist your peers to have similar conversations with your boss, the team effort might succeed without costing individuals too much. But if your colleagues get scared and back off, you could find yourself the only one with a thinner wallet.

Engage at a higher level

Pryce-Jones urges her coaching clients to learn everything possible about the company's new direction or strategy. Be curious. Ask good questions: Why has the strategy changed? What were the driving forces? And keep up with news about your industry. If you understand the larger context in which your company is operating, you'll better equip yourself to survive changes. "Be as proactive as you can as soon as you can," suggests leadership consultant Ron Ashkenas. "The more you can be part of the discussion, the more you can influence it."

Talking with your boss has already given you some perspective, but find out what pressures other departments face. Speak with other unit heads and peers with internal influence. It's entirely possible that your boss won't have any say in the specifics of the layoffs at all—higher-ups are making those decisions. So it's critical to make yourself known, in a positive way. The more perspectives you gather, the better informed you'll be. And if people can see that you're a curious, intelligent participant in conversations about the company's future, you'll increase your chances of being part of it.

Section 4
Build Your Skills

Chapter 13
Managing Conflict Constructively

When we think of conflict, often what comes to mind is war: factions diametrically opposed over a significant issue. But there are many types of conflicts. Not all of them are struggles for power or property or people. Lines are often drawn at work, too, and can sometimes be just as fiery: A colleague erupts in a meeting over a perceived injustice. Or a discussion grows heated and loud. But just because most workplaces are civil and quiet doesn't mean they're devoid of conflict.

Consider this story. Robin and Eli worked together on a joint project virtually, from different time zones. Robin spent her mornings drafting the piece of the project she'd be working on that day with Eli. When Eli came online several hours later, he wouldn't read what Robin had done; instead, he wanted to work together in real time to create a bullet-point outline. This practice annoyed Robin. Why had she spent hours getting a head start if

Build Your Skills

Eli was going to ignore her work and control the conversation later in the day anyway? She fell in line, ceding to his way of working, but she also started getting grumpy with him, growling at his suggestions or huffing her way through his re-creation of work she'd already done. This passive-aggressive dance went on for weeks, until finally Robin quit doing any work on the joint project. Eli didn't even notice that Robin had stopped contributing until she broke and flagged it for him. Sometimes, conflict is quiet.

It's also widespread. In fact, employees at all levels spend 2.8 hours a week dealing with unproductive conflict, according to a 2008 study by CPP Global. That adds up to more than $350 billion a year in wasted wages. *Unproductive conflict* might be as simple as experiencing a perceived slight or misunderstanding a process, as was the case with Robin. Or it could be as complicated as locking horns in a client presentation. We waste company time and money either entrenched in these fights or avoiding a confrontation while things get worse.

Work disputes not only prevent you from focusing on doing your job well but also likely bleed into your personal life, consuming your precious free time with worry, dumping misplaced frustration on your family, and placing unwelcome stress on you.

So why don't we have the argument and then move forward? In general, we avoid addressing uncomfortable issues because few people like to deal with conflict head-on. "People have a basic need to be liked," says leadership consultant Ron Ashkenas. "As soon as you get into a conflict, there's this discomfort that the relationship is going

112

to be broken." And on top of that fundamental human need, there are layers of complicated reasons that make it difficult to confront someone. Maybe you aren't sure where you fall in the informal hierarchy. Perhaps you've tried, and failed, to resolve clashes in the past. You could be secretly hoping that if you just wait it out, it will go away. Or maybe you imagine that your boss will notice and intervene.

But conflict is seldom resolved through avoidance or wishful thinking. Even the most conflict-averse of us can develop productive ways to confront—and resolve— thorny issues. The guidelines that follow will help you manage conflict more constructively.

Get More Comfortable with Conflict

First, you need to recognize that not all conflict is bad. In fact, it can be a healthy thing for an organization, leading to creativity, innovation, collaboration, and problem solving. Consider the classic tension between sales and product teams: Aggressive reps make customers promises that the product teams can't possibly deliver. Or so it seems—until the drive to satisfy the customer and meet expectations leads to innovations in manufacturing, product design, and sometimes completely new offerings.

"Teams composed of high-performing individuals are naturally subject to contradictory tensions, such as cooperation and rivalry," suggests Mark de Rond, an associate professor of strategy and organization at the Judge Business School, University of Cambridge, and the author of *There Is an I in Team*. But these tensions should not necessarily be managed away. They boost productivity and help teams perform better, because they stem from the group's same diversity of skills, approaches, and opinions that help it build a complete big-picture view, says de Rond, who has researched high-performing teams extensively.

But even if you recognize the benefits of different viewpoints and know that sometimes conflict leads to better work, how do you actually grow more comfortable with it?

Separate emotion from outcome

Consciously separate how you *feel* about the conflict from how it's affecting your work. It's possible that even though a situation seems tense to you, it's not actually interfering with excellent results, de Rond's research suggests. Participating in an after-action review of a failed product launch may raise your blood pressure, for example, but this discussion may also yield useful process changes to avoid such disasters in the future.

To help disentangle your feelings from your output, ask yourself whether your struggles with a colleague have actually had a negative impact. Have they made the project schedule slip, resulted in inferior work, or jeopardized a client relationship? It's not uncommon for work that *feels* difficult while it's under way to actually be stellar in the end—and recognizing this can help you see how tension is an integral part of the creative process.

Don't make it personal

You may also feel uncomfortable with conflict because you don't like the idea of "attacking" someone. But you can confront someone without shredding her character.

When you focus on the problem at hand, instead of the person involved, you can challenge a colleague without it sounding like—or being—an attack, advises Ashkenas. Asking probing questions and challenging assumptions, for example, and using language such as, "Have you thought about this?" and "Correct me if I'm wrong, but . . ." can go a long way toward shifting the conversation from "attack" to a calmer exploration of an issue. (For more on conducting difficult conversations, see chapter 14.)

When you focus on the outcome of your work and on whatever problems—not personality differences—there are, you'll grow more comfortable in confronting people, because it will feel less like they're out to get you or purposefully trying to make you crazy. Still, conflict is inevitable. Here's how to cope.

Identify and Resolve Your Conflict

Now that you've done some work on how you think about conflict, it's time to unearth the root cause of the tension at hand, find the courage to deal with it, and successfully work through the issue with your colleague. No matter what the source of conflict is, the key to resolving it is not to struggle in silence, says Ashkenas, but to bring your concern out in the open. "Try to make the implicit, explicit," he says. Name it. Say it out loud. Identify it for yourself first: "Nicolas and I have fundamentally different priorities on this project." A problem that is never articulated is unlikely to be solved—whether it's something you're harboring or your colleague is.

When you've collected your thoughts and cooled down from any anger or annoyance you were feeling, go see your colleague, privately, to discuss what's bothering you.

Ask him when a good time would be to meet. In essence you're asking for his permission to have a discussion, advises organizational development and HR expert Susan Heathfield. You can do it by e-mail or popping by his office. If your colleague isn't ready to have a discussion, he's likely to beg off: "Not today, I'm swamped." And then at least you know you need to give it a bit of time. But try again the next day. Don't go in with guns blazing; have your key points about your view of the differences, but be prepared to listen.

When you find a time that works for you, acknowledging the actual conflict will be an important start to solving it. Although situations vary, there are several universal pieces of advice for having a productive disagreement.

- **Articulate.** Understand and be able to clearly express what the clash is about.

- **Empathize.** Consider your colleague's point of view.

- **Have courage.** An honest conversation that recognizes your different perspectives will propel you forward.

Most disagreement stems from one of three sources, says Jeff Weiss, a partner at Vantage Partners consulting group and an expert in conflict management: different agendas, different perceptions, or different personal styles. Although many of the approaches offered here are broadly applicable, each of these three main sources has its own nuances that require attention. Here are suggestions for recognizing and navigating them.

Different agendas

When it comes to conflicts born of different agendas, we
often see well-intentioned people working toward different and legitimate aims who allow a situation to turn into
a black and white dispute: I want X. You want Y. We can't
agree. One of us has to lose for the other to win. This is
the most common source of disputes in a company, and it
isn't personal, Weiss says. You simply have different roles
and goals.

How can you find common ground despite these different goals? You need to sit down to talk with the other
person to figure out what you're each driving toward.

Tips on the conversation.

- **Explain what you're trying to achieve.** Express
  your desire to understand and be understood.
  Clarify that you're not after a battle of retorts. Say
  something such as, "I'm up against a hard dead-
  line, so trading e-mails back and forth is going to
  mean we lose the business, and it'll probably make
  us both unhappy in the process. Can we meet to
  discuss ways we might satisfy our client—and both
  of our needs?"

- **Ask your colleague what's at the root of his
  concern.** Really listen, and ask questions. Be open
  to his point of view. Genuinely try to grasp it. Using language such as, "May I ask why . . ." and "I'd
  like to hear what concerns you're trying to address

with . . ." will demonstrate that you're listening with an open mind.

- **Work with your colleague to come up with a better plan.** Now that you know what you're both working toward, is there a way to address both of your concerns and needs? Two well-intentioned people can usually work through their disagreement in any negotiation to get to a place they both feel good about. "Let's aim to get a revised proposal to the customer by the close of business tomorrow. Can we spend an hour together today working through language that might work for both of us?"

Let's see how a conflict of different agendas might unfold.

The wrong way.

Suppose you're a salesperson trying to close a large deal with a customer to meet your monthly goals. You've decided to offer a substantial discount and forgo the customary 25% deposit in advance of any work. This is a longtime customer, and you don't want to risk losing it to an aggressive new competitor. You try to slip the paperwork under the legal department's nose on a busy Friday so that it won't hold you up. But your colleagues are used to such frenzied month-end tactics. They know well the high price of poorly outlined terms that make it painful or impossible for finance to collect. They intercept the documents, calling out the deviations from standard contracts, and return a redlined nightmare that prevents you from closing the deal, serving your customer, and meeting your target.

A better way.

Explain what you're trying to achieve: "This is a longtime, reliable customer, and we've never had a problem with payment. I'm really worried that we're at risk of losing this substantial customer to a new competitor who is offering far more favorable terms. I'm trying to take some of the bureaucracy out of our agreement here to close a deal quickly and edge out our competitors." Empathize with your colleagues. What were they trying to achieve? "May I ask why you're leery of putting the contract through as it is? What concerns are you trying to address with your edits?" Get beyond accusations and ultimatums such as, "You can't do that" to discover what's motivating the behavior you don't like. The key to a productive outcome here is coming to an understanding of what's driving each other's agendas, says Weiss. When you learn more about why someone has a different view than you do—and you have a chance to explain your own—you're far more likely to find a creative solution that works for both of you.

Your goal isn't to "win" but to find a better way forward based on your increased comprehension of each other's interests. It may be that the legal department doesn't want a culture of one-off contract terms to become the norm. You may discover a new law that exposes your company to unseen liability if a particular clause is excluded from a contract. With an open conversation and brainstorming, you'll likely find a path that is better for the company.

Different perceptions

In conflicts that arise due to different perceptions, the basic facts are not in dispute, but what you think about those facts varies based on your personal filters. Two people can be in the same meeting and walk away with different ideas about what the next steps are. You just see the world differently. Resolving differences in perception, de Rond says, requires an explanation from both parties. Understanding your colleague's point of view—and how she came to it—and sharing how you came to yours will help you create a shared view.

Tips on the conversation.

- **Understand how you developed your own view.** Before you confront your colleague, Weiss advises, ask yourself, "What data, actions, or examples was I looking at that led to my conclusion?" Also ask "How am I interpreting this data? What meaning am I assigning to it?" It's possible your personal experiences or preferences have colored the information you received. Knowing what has shaped your perception will help you have a more productive conversation.

- **Ask your colleague how she reached her perception of the situation.** When you meet, have your colleague walk you through the data (it doesn't have to be quantitative), and the meaning that she gave to it, that led to her conclusion, suggests Weiss. You have two different pictures of what's going on that are both viable, and also likely quite understandable given your interpretations and experiences. Use open, nonconfrontational language. "Can you help me understand how you see . . .?" Listen to her side, without interrupting or debating.

- **Acknowledge that you have different perceptions.** Whether or not you agree with your colleague, acknowledge the difference in your views and explain that you realize why she reached her position. Doing so sets the right tone for a useful discussion. People are far more likely to come out of defensive mode when they feel they've been heard. Say, explicitly, "I might not agree with you, but I see why you came to that conclusion."

- **Share the thinking behind your own perspective.** This is your chance to rationally walk through why you've come to your point of view and to have a meaningful conversation. Because you were a good listener when your colleague was speaking, you've raised the odds for her to return the favor. If she tries to interrupt or dispute, a simple "Please hear me out" should help get the conversation back on track, advises Ashkenas. Keep the tone collegial and collaborative. Use language that acknowledges that you may not have all the answers. "You could be right, but I just wanted to talk through why I think it's important to . . ."

- **Allow your colleague to challenge you.** When you've both had a chance to air your views, it's time to discuss them. It's possible your perception feels wrong to the other person, so be open to hearing that. Give your colleague a chance to air whatever she has to say. Don't interrupt and defend yourself mid-sentence. Don't start building up your response in your mind before your colleague has finished. Force yourself to really listen to what she's saying. And when she's done, repeat to her what you think you heard, using neutral terms. "Do I have this right? You have consulted with a number of colleagues who feel that this particular project is different from previous ones and needs more input than normal. And my suggestions are not taking that into account?" If your colleague hears it come back to her accurately, then she opens up the possibility of listening closely to you. You've both shifted into neutral. If your colleague clams up—her hostile body language the only indicator—solicit her challenge. "I'm guessing you disagree. Can you tell me what you're thinking?"

- **Come to a third point of view.** It may be that neither of you is able to agree with the other person's perspective, but at least you'll know why you disagree. And your conversations may then lead to a third, alternative view.

Here's how a conflict of perceptions might play out in real life.

The wrong way.

Say you and your colleague Rohit are asked to join the team that will redesign your company's website. The

CEO's mandate is to create a high-quality web presence using the best internal resources possible. But what does "best internal resources possible" mean? You think it entails targeting resources—getting internal buy-in on key aspects related to function. As such, you're willing to risk delaying the launch so that finance, sales, and marketing are happy with the shopping cart functionality. But Rohit seems to be interpreting "best internal resources possible" to mean that *everyone* needs to weigh in on the look and feel of the new site. Rather than giving formal presentations to keep folks up-to-date on how the redesign is coming together, he's conducting one-on-one sessions with random people—for instance, asking finance colleagues what they think about color palettes or fonts. His seemingly whimsical feedback collection strategy threatens to delay the schedule, and for what purpose? Needless niceties of tapping a group that has no expertise in this area? The CEO put you both on the team because you're known for bringing difficult projects in on time. But you're steaming over Rohit's approach, whereas he thinks the approach you're advocating excludes employee input.

You confront Rohit: "Enough with the cube-by-cube tour of wireframes! You're more concerned with looking like a superhero project manager of the people than you are about the impact all this feedback will have on the people who actually need to implement and act on it." He's genuinely shocked and hurt. The way he sees it, he's been following the CEO's orders to use company resources, gathering input and keeping a complex project on track. How did you get to such different places?

A better way.

Assume that your colleague has good reason for his different opinion; it's unlikely he's working just to spite you. Ask him to explain how he sees the issue, and then you should have the same opportunity. Digging into what you each think something means (what does "best use of internal resources" look like to you?) will help you both better manage your expectations and future behavior. "Can you help me identify which presentations you thought were important, and which ones you decided to pass on?" Listen to his reply. It could be, for example, that Rohit's informal conversations with people in the finance department suggested that they'd rather not sit through an hour-long PowerPoint presentation and preferred to offer their recommendations in a more ad hoc format. You don't have to agree with his view, but you should acknowledge it: "I can see why you wound up chatting with the finance folks one-on-one, given their schedule constraints." Then share what's behind your perspective: "Let me explain why I think it's important to consult people from different departments only on their area of expertise."

It may be that neither of you is able to agree with the other person's perspective, but at least you'll know why you disagree. And your conversations may then lead to an alternative view. Together, you can craft a productive solution: The two of you could cohost town-hall-style meetings to targeted groups, but make attendance voluntary. You could then send summary briefings to the core team members for their feedback before they finalize decisions—all well within the bounds of your schedule.

Different personal styles

Type A personality versus creative maverick. Deadline-driven person versus a "schedules are only guidelines" type. Conflicts born of different personal styles can be the most difficult to navigate, because at their core, it might be that you and your colleague are completely different. But as with the other two sources of disagreement, your primary goal is to see where your colleague is coming from and what is motivating his request or behavior, says Weiss. Understanding, appreciating, and trying to take advantage of your different views will help you move forward.

Tips on the conversation.

- **Give your colleague the benefit of the doubt.**
"Make the starting point in your mind the assumption that the other person isn't intentionally trying to screw you," Ashkenas advises. Most people are trying to do their jobs the best way they know how. Your colleague's behavior has nothing to do with you. He's probably like this with everyone. It's just how he operates.

- **Acknowledge that there are differences—and identify them.** Recognize that the core issue might simply be a different way of thinking. Articulate what you perceive to be the central differences. It can't simply be that she "bugs" you. (And if someone grates on you, you probably don't have grounds for an air-clearing conversation with her. Take a walk around the block instead. See chapter 15, "Working with People You Just Can't Stand.") Name the specific *behavior* or *actions* that you disagree with: "You and I seem to have a different view on when meetings start. I expect the meeting to start at 9 if we've called it for 9. But you seem to think the meeting doesn't really start until everyone is there."

- **Find a way forward.** When you have both perspectives on the table, together you can find a solution without rehashing past offenses or pointing fingers. To do that effectively, frame the conversation toward the future: If you spend your time picking over "he said, she said" analysis, you'll never get anywhere. Mary Shapiro, management consultant and author of the *HBR Guide to Leading Teams,* suggests asking the question, "What do we need to do differently going forward?" For instance, what reporting relationships need to change? What time lines? What team processes? How can you or others change the context to prevent unhelpful behavior going forward? How would you like to work with your colleague in the future?

A real-life conflict of personal styles might look like this.

The wrong way.

Say you're a punctual person. You make a point of being on time or early to every meeting you attend or facilitate. You come prepared, you've put away unnecessary electronics, and you don't get caught up in small talk that eats away at planned meeting time. Your colleague Alan, on the other hand, routinely turns up to meetings 10 minutes late. He breezes in, all apologies, and then looks expectantly at you as facilitator to bring him up to speed. Everyone who arrived on time endures a re-hashing of material they covered only minutes ago. The people in the meeting roll their eyes at you for not being sensitive to their time, and you're mentally throttling Alan. Everyone's frustrated, and now you're behind on your agenda, too.

The next time Alan turns up late for your meeting, you dramatically stop the discussion and make a spectacle of his tardiness: "Alan, how *nice* of you to join us!" Or perhaps you begin overloading his inbox with excessive meeting reminders, hovering near his desk when it's time to head to the conference room. You're so focused on your annoyance with him, you don't pay attention to the five other people who consistently turn up for your meetings on time and prepared.

A better way.

When your conflict is the result of a clash of personal styles, take a moment to remind yourself that people who are different from each other can still get along. Think about what's really bothering you. When you've collected your thoughts and emotions, meet with your colleague to learn more about where he's coming from and to find a way to work together. You might say, "Alan, I'm frustrated when you're late for meetings, because I feel that we either can't start without you or if we do start, we'll need to pause and bring you up to speed. Is there something I can do to schedule them in a way that works better for you?" He may reveal a very good reason for consistently being late to meetings. Perhaps he assumes that you know he's in meetings so much of the day that it's physically impossible to finish one meeting at noon and be in his seat for the next one by 12:01. Or he may have seen from the agenda that the first five minutes would be an overview of the project—really for the benefit of the more junior employees—and that his contributions would be needed when you were further along the agenda. Once you've both shared your perspectives, you can work toward a solution. For example, you might conclude that Alan will take a narrower role in the meeting. You remain leader, and he joins the group at an agreed-upon time to serve as an expert on a key issue. Or you could let him know when it's particularly important that he attend a meeting so that he can rearrange his schedule or commitments to be on time.

There are many shades of gray in those three broad types of discord, so it's no wonder it can seem easier to just avoid having a confrontation. But analyzing what's driving the tension can help you ameliorate it. If you're prepared to walk through the steps of understanding what the disagreement is about, giving your colleague the benefit of the doubt, and hashing out a better way forward without creating "winners" and "losers," you'll genuinely be developing your skills as a collaborator and colleague whom people respect.

Know When to Bring In the Boss

As a last resort, it's OK to escalate a problem with a colleague to your boss, says Weiss, but only after you've given some real thought to why you two haven't been able to resolve the problem on your own. Most managers aren't interested in fighting your battles for you. But if everything you've tried together has failed, enlist the other person in the escalation to avoid looking as if you're "tattling." In a calm moment, go to your colleague and see if you can at least jointly define the problem and diagnoses for it to better help your manager help you.

Acknowledge that you're both trying to do the right thing; you just happen to disagree on what that is, and admit that you're at a standstill. "John, I don't think you and I are getting anywhere trying to resolve this issue. Would you be willing to go with me to ask Lydia for her help in working through a solution?" Transparency builds trust.

Agree that you'll reach out to the boss together, and work out the specifics: Will the two of you stop by to ask her to meet with you? Will you send an e-mail invitation that you both draft and are copied on? Approaching the boss in this way sends a clear message that you're cooperating in your quest for a solution.

It's in your mutual interest to avoid being seen as difficult to work with or unwilling to compromise. When you meet with the boss, explain that you seem to have different objectives (or work styles, or perceptions) and that you're at an impasse. This is not an opportunity to complain about the other person—either directly or through passive-aggressive language (such as "*John* seems to think that it's worth risking losing a key customer in order to keep the historic blueprint of all our contracts intact").

Instead, state the issue clearly, focusing on the problem, not the personalities: "We're stuck, and we need your help thinking this through." Frame the conflict by describing its impact on the organization. "This customer is worth $10 million in business to us annually. We want to be careful not to establish a bad precedent for overlooking important legal protections, but if we can't agree on the right language for this contract quickly, we risk the customer looking elsewhere." Briefly explain what you've tried thus far. Your neutral airing of the issue, your united front in appearing at the meeting, and your demonstration of how you've tried to solve the problem will make your boss more willing to work with you both. She may know of other internal resources—such as in-house mediation services or organizational guidelines for conflict. Or she may just make a judgment call that you both have to live with.

Finding productive ways to work through conflict with your colleagues offers tremendous benefits: a unified front for working with customers or suppliers, faster and better internal decision making, reduced costs through sharing resources and expertise, and the development of more innovative products and solutions, Weiss points out.

As you grow more comfortable with conflict and your resolution skills improve over time, your boss and colleagues will come to respect the way you work collaboratively through obstacles. Some of the greatest leaders in history have excelled by navigating conflict effectively. Abraham Lincoln, for example, famously brought his rivals into his inner circle. According to de Rond, "I think workplaces today place far too much emphasis on harmony in teams, assuming that the better you and I get along, the better we will perform. Most teams that I have studied have not been easy places to be for a lot of the time. But they were effective." Choosing to be effective involves working through conflict. It's a skill that can help drive your own performance and career to a much better place.

Chapter 14
Conducting Difficult Conversations

Many of us find ourselves in professional situations when we believe someone has wronged us, just plain made us mad, or treated us badly. The advice often given by the experts in this book is to have the courage to have an honest conversation; air the grievance. No one can help you solve a problem if she doesn't know you have it. But that's easier said than done, right?

We've gathered advice from some of the world's top thinkers on communication challenges in the workplace. If you have a strategy for difficult conversations before you need one, you're far more likely to get through them successfully. Here's how.

Why We Avoid Difficult Conversations

Why are we afraid to face a conversation even if it has the potential to make things better for us? It's because we fear what we might lose more than we want what we might gain. "It goes to the nature of who we are as human beings," says Cornell professor Jim Detert, who has researched why employees are often afraid to speak up in organizations. "We have deep financial, material well-being concerns. We have deep, deep social concerns. Fear of ostracism is one of the biggest fears humans have. At the deepest level, that's why people are afraid to challenge their colleagues." We fear so much: losing the respect of our colleague, spiraling out of control in the moment, being proven wrong, getting pushed aside or fired for not going along with the status quo. Detert also says that it's human nature to disproportionately remember times we've spoken up (or witnessed someone speaking up) and it's gone wrong, amplifying that fear.

It can be so overwhelming that many of us try everything we can to put it off or avoid it altogether. Some people would rather *change jobs* than actually attempt to directly confront a colleague or manager about something that's bothering them. But "while it's completely human to have a tendency to delay," observes INSEAD's Jean-François Manzoni, "a delay is largely unproductive. The dynamic gets worse. You think you're hiding your aggravation, but you're not. The other party will sense something's wrong, and that's probably not going to help."

But if you find ways to navigate difficult conversations, your colleagues will come to respect your candor and your ability to work through a problem without making it personal. And when you conduct difficult conversations, you're contributing to an environment where having hard talks, offering different points of view, and giving honest feedback are accepted—and that is better for everyone and for your organization as a whole.

How to Have a Productive Conversation

There's no one-strategy-fits-all approach to challenging conversations, but there are guiding principles. The process should proceed in two phases: the preparation you do, if you can, to set yourself up for success; and then the navigation of the actual conversation. If the two of you aren't able to work things out on your own, there may be organizational resources you can lean on.

Prepare

Although most people might focus on changing how they feel and act *during* a confrontation, Manzoni says it's more important to prepare before you have the conversation. "My experience is that 75% of the battle is fought before you walk into the room," says Manzoni, who has conducted extensive research on conflict management. The most effective things you can do, Manzoni says, are to manage your own state of mind and consider how you'll frame the conversation. To psych yourself up for a difficult, but positive, chat, follow these guidelines.

Manage the timing.

You want to avoid delaying a difficult conversation just because you dread it, but sometimes choosing *not* to have it is the right call, says Jeanne Brett, director of Kellogg School of Management's Dispute Resolution Research Center. If you're so angry that you can't control your emotions, you're not in a good frame of mind for a discussion. "In the heat of the moment, it's important to recognize 'I'm in no emotional shape to have this conversation,'" she observes. You'll say the wrong thing, embarrass yourself or your colleague, or create awkward scenes for others. In those instances, she advises, it's wiser to take time to cool down. Walk around the building. Change your surroundings, and work in a small conference room or head home to work in peace there.

If your colleague confronts you in the hallway after a meeting or walks into your office ready to explode, Brett suggests you do whatever you can to put off the conversation. "I see that this is a problem, and I'd like to take some time to think about ways to resolve it. I promise I'll come by your office tomorrow to discuss it." Acknowledge your colleague's feelings—"I can see you're really upset about this"—and then ask whether you can set a time to talk when you're both calmer. "It's tough not to be defensive in such a situation, especially if you were caught off guard," Brett advises. (For more on confrontations, see chapter 13, "Managing Conflict Constructively.")

When you're ready, find a good time to talk to your colleague. Not first thing on Monday when you're both coming in to a full inbox. Not last thing on Friday when you're eager for the weekend to begin. Instead, find a time and place that are least likely to add tension to the meeting. Right after lunch in a neutral conference room? Over coffee at the local greasy spoon? Avoid "turf" settings; inviting people into your office for a conversation gives you home field advantage, because it's filled with your professional mementos, you're the one sitting behind a desk (and usually in a larger chair, signaling your higher power), and so on, Detert advises. Ideally you'll find a time and place where you'll both feel up to working through a healthy conversation.

Manage your message.

What do you want your counterpart to take away from the conversation? You'll have a better chance of being heard if you define your message and decide how you'll convey it.

- **Articulate your goal.** Ask yourself what you're trying to achieve with the conversation, suggests Manzoni. Does what you want make sense? Is it realistic? If not, let it go and set your sights a little lower.

- **Identify a constructive frame.** Considering how you'll approach the conversation—literally what you'll say and won't say—will set you up to succeed. View it as a presentation: What information does your partner need to hear? Identify the key points you'd like to make, highlighting mutual benefits when possible.

- **Consider your colleague's point of view.** Before (and during) the conversation, try to get a sense of what your colleague might be thinking. She made her choices or behaved in a certain way for a reason. What might that reason be? How might she respond to your approach? Also ask yourself whether there's any other explanation for what's bothering you. Is your take on the situation fair? Ask a colleague for his interpretation of the events to see whether your conclusions are reasonable. Paint the situation for him as neutrally as you can. Cataloging every fault and misstep will probably get you sympathy but not constructive feedback, so focus on the problem.

With your emotions and thoughts collected, and an appointment on the calendar, you're ready to talk.

During the conversation

Whether your discussion happens unexpectedly or it's something you've scheduled, these guidelines will help you as you conduct it.

- **Make it two-way.** Maintain the most positive, open, and constructive mind-set you can. "Don't assume that the other party is unreasonable," advises Manzoni. Walk into the room "as present in the moment as possible. Be prepared to listen to what is being said—or not being said." If you have something to say that might not be easy for others to hear, recognize that there are other points of view, while presenting your thoughts as part of a conversation. In this way, people will be far more likely to *hear* you rather than shut down. According to Detert, using language that acknowledges that everyone's view, including your own, is a "partial view"—such as "I understand the current thinking is X, but I'd like to share my view and hear yours"—is far more conducive to an open, nondefensive conversation.

- **Focus on the problem, and not the personalities.** You may feel as though someone repeatedly disrespects you, but just airing that isn't likely to solve your disagreement. When you focus on the *problem,* and not the person, you're less likely to get your colleague's defenses up and so you're more likely to have a good outcome. Camille may never read your reports even though you worked hard to write them well and on time, but the larger problem is that when she fails to read the reports, she isn't up to speed on what your group is doing, and that could lead to conflicts or mistakes down the line. Highlighting the impact of her behavior is a better approach than telling her it annoys you: "I'm adding a lot of details that you might not be aware of in my reports to you. I'm concerned that if you aren't finding time to read them routinely, then you and I aren't in sync. Is there a better way for me to keep you informed?"

- **Accept responsibility.** Americans, in particular, says Brett, tend to want to point to factors beyond their personal control when something goes wrong: "Liam's team never responded when I asked for updates." But that's the last thing any boss wants to hear. You're more likely to infuriate him and suggest that you can't handle responsibility. If you are part of the problem, say so up front.

Even if it's not really your fault, "own" the problem: "I know you wanted this to come in on budget, but I didn't manage to make that happen." Your boss may well be angry with the news—and in fairness, you have to allow him the opportunity to express that anger—but there's little for him to stew on if you've clearly accepted responsibility and addressed concerns so that it won't happen again.

- **Propose solutions.** Don't merely scratch at a problem. Flag it, and then show up at the meeting with ideas on how you can fix whatever is going wrong. Be a problem solver: "I know we ran over budget, but I have two ideas for how we can cut costs on the next phase of the project to help mitigate that. And I've discussed with the other team members how we can avoid the problem next time."

- **Forget winners and losers; stay in neutral.** Conversations that depend on one party admitting complete defeat—"You're right, I was totally wrong"—aren't likely to be successful. "People think difficult conversations have winners and losers, so they try to win," observes Holly Weeks, author of *Failure to Communicate: How Conversations Go Wrong and What You Can Do to Right Them.* But a better outcome is for both parties to win. To do this, set a neutral tone from the beginning. "I might say, 'Karen, I have something difficult to talk about. It's hard for me, and I think it's going to be hard for you because it's something we haven't talked about yet,'" suggests Weeks. This is a problem identification and problem solving conversation, and not a battle. "Neutral is a nice, easy formula. Clear content, neutral tone, tempered phrasing." Your face, your body, and your voice should shift into (or stay in) neutral. Don't yield to the temptation to escalate, respond in anger, or give in to your colleague unnecessarily.

- **Take the temperature.** During your difficult conversation, pause for a moment to check your view of where things are. This isn't a time for sweeping characterizations: "I know we're really far apart on this." Rather, Weeks advises stopping to take stock in a sincere and collegial way: "Here's where I think we're more or less on the same page" and "Here's where I think we're not." Giving yourselves a moment to assess where your disagreement stands may well speed things along.

Explore organizational resources

You don't want to escalate a dispute too quickly, but sometimes people get so entrenched in their positions, or situations get so heated, that you can't work it out on your own. If that happens to you, don't give up hope just yet.

Consider recruiting a neutral third party—maybe a manager or a respected colleague. Explain the conflict, indicate the impact on your group or the organization, and ask whether your colleague is willing to get involved. You're not after that person to pick sides, but rather to provide a neutral space and time for the two of you to talk more rationally. Your neutral colleague could approach the other party, at your request, to organize a private sit-down: "Look, I know you and so-and-so have been wrestling with this issue. Can we sit down in my office and talk about it? It's starting to affect the entire department."

Your company may also provide low-key solutions for difficult conversations. Are there in-house mediators? Will HR staff act as sounding boards? What organizational rules or aspects of your company culture can help you work through your difficult conversation? If your company is mission driven, can "quality in everything you do" help you and your partner refocus your argument? Is there a company ombudsman who can listen and offer a neutral perspective without its becoming an official conversation?

Difficult Conversations in the Real World

It helps to have guiding principles to call on when you need to work through something difficult. But the context of your discussion also matters. Do you need to take a stand on something? Deliver bad news? Do you have time to prepare, or are you caught off guard? Here are some specific tips for navigating common scenarios.

If you have to deliver bad news . . .

No one likes to deliver bad news, especially to your boss. While your instinct might be to try to soft-pedal the news or hide it, experts say that's the worst possible thing you can do. Here we see the power of problem solving in defusing an unpleasant conversation.

The wrong way.

Avoid the conversation. Or e-mail the boss after work hours, when she can't come and find you: "I just wanted to update you that we made a mistake in the printed edition of the magazine. It's too late to fix it."

A better way.

Admit that there's a problem, figure out what went wrong, take responsibility, and propose a solution. "When I was editor of a prestigious trade magazine, I realized that we had stupidly published a provocative letter to the editor from a very famous person—that turned out to be a completely fake letter," recalls a journalist. "We only realized this when we got an angry call from that famous person. And my boss was a notorious hothead. This would be a major embarrassment for the magazine."

What did the editor do? Precisely what the experts suggest: "I figured out exactly how the mistake had happened. My assistant was supposed to confirm all the letters, but she was new and she didn't know how to contact the famous person. So she didn't." Then the editor designed a new procedure to guarantee that such a mistake wouldn't happen again. She went into her boss's office to tell him as quickly as she could so that he didn't hear about it from other channels. He blew his stack, but then they were able to have a good conversation. "I took complete responsibility—it was ultimately my fault. I let him blow steam at me. And then I presented him with a solution." The boss was mad, but the conversation ended in that one session.

If you're mad about a decision that affects you . . .

We've all had white-hot reactions to news that affects our jobs. But nothing good comes from launching from your chair to give your boss or colleague a piece of your mind: You'll lose the argument before you open your mouth. But waiting until you're calm, and framing how the decision is bad for the company—and not just you—will put you on a more productive path, says Brett.

The wrong way.

"I just found out that Peter got double the raise I got. Are you *kidding* me? I work three times as hard as he does! WTF?"

A better way.

Take a broader view of the issue. If you're unhappy about a decision, might others be, too? If so, why? What's the larger issue for your team or organization? Brett advises framing the conversation as, "I've observed something that's not good for the company, and I'd like to help address it" rather than "I'm really mad this decision has been made about me." After discovering that her peer received a much larger raise, a young partner in a law firm successfully employed Brett's approach of framing the problem as an organization-wide challenge. Although the young partner was upset, she recognized that it wouldn't be wise to complain about her colleague's raise or ruminate about the injustice. The firm hadn't deliberately set out to slight her; another partner had just made a more convincing case for raising her colleague's pay. So the aggrieved lawyer approached the senior partner, making clear that she didn't begrudge her colleague's raise, but framed the issue as one of lack of transparency: "We don't have a clear, fair system for raises in this firm." She volunteered to do some research on how other firms handled the same challenge so that her organization could create a better process. Eventually that research led to a new, fair, transparent system, one the partner was happy with. Although she didn't get a salary correction immediately, she improved her situation for the future—and created a better process for everyone.

If you need to make critical comments in a public forum . . .

Speaking up is challenging enough. But speaking out in front of everyone in your company? It's fodder for nightmares. Still, it doesn't have to be. Preparing thoroughly, framing the issue with a company focus, and positioning yourself as a problem solver will help make the daunting task of raising concerns at a large meeting, such as a board meeting or all-staff meeting, more palatable and productive.

The wrong way.

It's unwise to make a statement like this in front of everyone: "I think this is a stupid idea for the company. If we keep proceeding down this path, prepare for a death spiral!"

A better way.

Before you stand up, prepare to take some heat. Making a critical comment in a public forum is likely to generate anger in people who don't agree with you. So say explicitly that you're trying to do what you think is best for the company. But also recognize, Brett says, that you're probably not alone: "In every case, you're not likely to be the only person who has these concerns." If possible, find a like-minded colleague before the meeting who might be prepared to back you up.

To start the conversation, say something like, "I know everyone thinks we can manage the potential conflict of interest between these clients, but I feel very strongly that if we start down this path, we'll find ourselves managing all kinds of conflicts that will be destructive to our customers down the line." But don't stop there. Identify potential solutions to the problem you're raising. "I know this will delay our work for the client, but I'm happy to spend the next few days discussing some alternative paths forward with other folks." Hopefully one or two of your colleagues will join you in voicing the importance of alternative paths and volunteer to study the issue with you.

If a colleague goes postal on you . . .

Do not respond to raw anger. Let your colleague's words wash over you. See whether the scene will wind down. Here's where managing your thoughts and emotions will help you navigate this challenge successfully. "Most people reciprocate other people's behavior," Brett says. "It takes discipline not to get angry in response. But it's effective."

The wrong way.

"What are you talking about?! You have no idea what work went into this project! Next time I'm not going to bother to ask your opinion!"

A better way.

You don't need to go all the way to the other extreme and cower, or apologize for something you didn't do, but you can simply choose not to engage in the battle. If your colleague is so emotional that you can't get a word in edgewise, sometimes merely labeling the situation helps de-escalate the tension: "Listen, we can trade threats and insults here, but that's not going to solve our problem. We're not getting anywhere this way." You're much better off removing yourself from a situation than trying to fight back. Suggest you meet later to discuss the problem. Do whatever you need to do to stay calm and avoid having an emotional conversation.

But because you can't always dictate the timing—and trying to do so can make some people even angrier as they stew about the problem—it helps to respond in the most neutral way possible without conceding or escalating. Neutral in this case sounds like this: "I don't know what to say. This is unexpected. What shall we do next?" suggests Weeks. You haven't placated the person, you haven't conceded; instead, you have calmly acknowledged that your colleague is angry. The conversation may not be pleasant after that, but you haven't made anything worse for either of you. You're now thinking together, rather than just reacting.

On the other hand, if you *are* in the wrong, and you know it, apologize immediately, says Weeks. "I'm sorry. I meant that to be funny." That's it, you're done. Don't keep piling on the explanation. Just own it.

It's not (often) possible to magically make a difficult conversation fun and happy and easy. That's why they're challenging. But you can make them more productive by preparing yourself to get through them better. The only way you're going to get better at navigating difficult conversations, says Weeks, is to have them. "You're not going to get more skillful if what you do is step aside from the issue," she says. And worse, the issue that you think you're sidestepping isn't likely to go away, setting up you or your colleague for a disproportionate blowup. Difficult conversations are *difficult*, says Weeks. But that doesn't mean you can't get better at them by preparing, staying neutral, and focusing on a solution that's not only better for you but also better for the company.

Chapter 15
Working with People You Just Can't Stand

When you think of your dream team, you imagine the exact roster of people you'd like to work with—hand-picked for compatibility and talent. But unfortunately, that's not how the real world works. Instead, you're likely to be working alongside one or two people whom you just don't like. At all. Not even a little bit. Maybe your colleague simply rubs you the wrong way. He's loud. Or a suck-up. Or arrogant and entitled. Perhaps he's courteous and professional in front of the boss, but a nightmare to you and your colleagues when she's not around. Or maybe he has mannerisms that annoy you (relentless pen clicking!).

There's no shortage of good reasons you might genuinely dislike someone you need to work with. Sometimes they're legitimate (she avoids established protocols to get "special" treatment for her work), and sometimes they're not (he's still clicking that pen!). But unless the person is crossing serious ethical or legal boundaries of what's acceptable at work—such as sexual harassment—you must find a way to coexist. If you don't, your own performance is likely to suffer. But wait, you're not the creep: How does his behavior have a negative effect on your work?

When you have unaddressed negative feelings for a colleague, it can cause all sorts of issues for you. It can consume you so that you neglect to focus on doing good work. You might decline signing on to an otherwise appealing project because you can't stand the thought of collaborating with him. Or you might suppress your annoyance for so long that it builds and bursts over a minor infraction—leaving you looking unstable. You could subconsciously mirror the attitude you sense from him, becoming a jerk yourself. In any case, getting swept up in power struggles can be a waste of time.

Anger, avoidance, and sabotage are all paths to failure. On the other hand, working with colleagues you like and respect is important for your job satisfaction—and for office morale. If you can't have office mates you like, you need to find a way to like the colleagues you have—or at least not *dislike* them. Learning to get along with everyone can have long-term benefits for your career; if the person you can't stand is in your industry, chances are you'll run into him again at events or through your network, even if your prayers are answered and he leaves your company. Maintaining a positive connection is much more beneficial than just breathing a sigh of relief.

But how can you learn to work effectively with someone you just can't stand? It's not always possible to make the situation better, concedes Ben Dattner, author of *The Blame Game*. But it is possible to make things worse through a wrong-headed response. Our experts offer the following strategies to improve your chances of getting it right.

Examine and Adjust Your Perspective

Throughout this book, our experts have advised that a good first step for many political situations is to begin with self-reflection. How does this advice apply here? "You've got to start from a place where you understand that every person is different and everyone brings in different strengths," advises organizational development and HR expert Susan Heathfield. "So if you're seeing behaviors you can't stand in someone, ask yourself, 'What is *my* problem that I'm having such a hard time with this person?'" The easiest way to survive working with someone you really don't like is to choose not to let that person bother you. You have little control over someone else. The only thing you can control is your own response to whatever annoying behaviors she directs your way. Here's how.

Look in the mirror

"There's lots of evidence that we, as human beings, are incredibly blind to our own weakness," says Stanford professor Bob Sutton, author of *The No Asshole Rule*. So consider how you might be contributing to the problem. Try to objectively assess what you may have done to escalate tensions. Or ask a colleague for her perspective. The goal, says Sutton, is to test your assumptions. Sometimes what you're reacting to has little to do with the other person and more to do with your own history, says Dattner.

It's possible that the person reminds you of an obnoxious sibling or a high school rival. Or maybe you can be a bit of a control freak, and your frustration comes more from being unable to direct your colleague than from his actual actions.

Identifying your own emotional influences is important, Dattner says, because it means you can manage your impulses. When confronted by the prospect of working with someone you dislike, consider the history of your relationship. Did it start out good and get bad? Try to identify why exactly you don't like this person. Did she do something to trigger your reaction, or do you just somehow bring out the worst in each other? Work to isolate what's keeping you from being less than your best self. If you still can't see it, identify what your healthy professional relationships have in common—and work on trying to build that quality in this one.

Get to know the person you despise

Sometimes the root of the issue is that you just don't know or understand the other person. "You have to distinguish between people you don't know who you think are idiots—and people you are genuinely locked in conflict with," says Sutton. Give him the benefit of the doubt. Communication and branding expert Dorie Clark suggests finding ways to work with someone you don't like as a way of getting better insight into the person he is and what he has to offer. Give him a chance to excel at something he's good at. Clark once suggested that she and a disliked colleague go rock climbing as a way of improving their relationship. Clark was a novice, but her colleague was an experienced climber. "Seeing him comfortable, more laid back, and responsible made me see a different side of him," she recalls. Although they didn't suddenly become best buddies, it was helpful for her to see him in a more positive light. People often complain that they don't like working or collaborating with a colleague, says Dattner, until they see him out of the office, at an off-site event. "This is eye-opening" for many people, he says. When we see our colleagues as three-dimensional—they have families and friends and interests outside work—it's often the opening to finding them more pleasant to work with.

Once you know a little bit more about who he is, it can be easier to imagine where he's coming from. "People also tend to like people better when they've actually collaborated with them on something," says Sutton. So don't shy away from working with someone you *think* you don't like. Sometimes being in the trenches on a difficult project can be a powerful bonding experience that just might change your opinion.

Cultivate empathy

Even if your colleague is doing something that genuinely annoys you, putting yourself in her shoes will help you comprehend what's behind her behavior. And if you can see that, you're more likely to find ways to work through your issues. For example, if you find that a coworker seems to be hostile in every meeting in which you're discussing future strategy for the company, consider why she might be acting that way. Is it possible she hasn't felt consulted about a decision? Were her ideas rejected or ignored? Imagine if you had worked for months on a proposal of new markets for the company and no one had even bothered to acknowledge it. Empathy—understanding what's driving someone's feelings—gives you insight that can help you fix what's wrong.

Someone may bug you on a personal level, but that doesn't mean the person isn't an asset to the company. "Assume the best, focus on what they're good at, and how they can help your team," says Sutton. Take time to think about the value this person brings to your company. Sure, he guffaws at his own jokes, but maybe he's also great with spreadsheets. Perhaps his jokes have a way of easing your boss's tension and keeping him calm. Maybe his persnickety report-reviewing highlights your terrible typing skills, but it also brings to light a major accounting error that would have cost the company a significant loss of revenue. Actively search for what you can legitimately admire about him.

When a new colleague rubbed Akiko the wrong way, she found herself bristling at his arrogance. Colby was quick to get frustrated with others if they didn't immediately warm to his ideas. He'd aggressively declare that whatever he was proposing was brilliant, as if to suggest that Akiko and everyone else there was dumb for not seeing it. After finally snapping at Colby in a meeting, Akiko pulled him aside to apologize. "I said, 'When you push your ideas like that, it makes me feel stupid if I don't get it right away. Sometimes I just need to understand more about what you're suggesting.'" Colby was aghast that his arguments would be seen that way. It turned out, Colby's enthusiasm for his ideas often got in the way of his ability to communicate clearly, and then he got more frustrated with himself when other people didn't quite follow. After their frank conversation, the problem disappeared. Akiko would say, "Let me ask you a few questions about that" as a way of signaling that she wasn't following, and Colby would realize that she was helping him articulate his ideas.

Deal Directly with a Jerk

If your attempts at getting to the root of your own feelings (as well as those of your colleague) haven't changed the game enough for you, you'll need a different strategy for dealing with someone you can't stand. Sutton suggests steeling yourself for two possible—and opposite—approaches.

Change the dynamic

If you've allowed yourself to get into a negative pattern with the person you just can't stand, "you need to disrupt the cycle," Clark says. Be conscious of how *you* treat her. Are you civil to her? Does your voice stay calm? Do you roll your eyes? Your behavior may have helped make the dislike mutual. "It's possible they're negative because they sense your hostility," Clark notes. "If you alter the dynamic by shifting from subtly hostile to actively positive, they may respond in kind."

How can you change seemingly unconscious negative reactions? Take the high road. It's hard for someone to be annoyed with someone who's being nice to them, Sutton says. So be helpful. When she sends out a proposal, be one of the first people to read and reply. Praise the person's ideas (when you *genuinely* think they're good). Mention to a colleague or your manager when the person has done something notable, even if she never hears that you did so. Inviting a colleague to be part of the process, and then seeking her input, can dramatically change the dynamic of a tense relationship. For example, project manager Kate might accept a schedule change if she's part of the brainstorming meeting that decides the priorities for finishing the project.

Fight back

If you come to realize that you're never going to be able to stop the annoying behavior *or* your reaction to it, you don't have to just accept that's how it is, Sutton says. Ranting to other colleagues in search of sympathy and allies may earn *you* the title of difficult colleague. But you can take your issue directly to the colleague with whom you're not getting along.

Heathfield suggests giving your annoying colleague a heads-up that you have something to discuss with him. "I'd like to give you some feedback about how I think we can better work together. Would tomorrow at two o'clock be a good time?" Don't blindside him. Someone who gets on your nerves under the most benign circumstance is not likely to react well if you catch him off guard by sharing feedback or criticism in the hallway. As you've seen in dealing with bullies—and having difficult conversations—you'll want to focus your conversation on the problem and not the person. So think about the specific behaviors that are bothering you as you prepare for your meeting.

Begin the conversation by clarifying that your intention is to find a good way forward. Heathfield advises saying something like, "I really want to work effectively with you—that's my goal. But I've felt that that isn't possible at the moment. Here are a few of the reasons that I'm feeling that way." Don't use labels: "I think you're being a jerk when . . ." or "You're so aggressive." Instead, stick to the facts: "Here are the behaviors that I'm observing." Now, Heathfield says, at least you've opened a discussion that might clear the air or bring you to a better place of mutual empathy. In many instances, the person knows he's been acting badly, but he didn't think anyone would notice. "Sometimes when you confront them, it's like, 'Oh my god, she caught me! I was doing these things, but I didn't think she knew.'" Other times, you'll discover there's a perfectly innocent explanation for your colleague's actions. "I've been hypercritical because I know that the C-level guys are going to run our department through intense scrutiny. I want to make sure we hold up well." Or, often, "I really had no idea. I didn't mean to be offensive."

Keep your cool throughout the conversation. Don't be snide or insulting or mean, even if your colleague isn't taking your feedback well. "Imagine in any given conversation that everyone else in the workplace is listening," advises Dattner. "Would I want this clip to be on YouTube?" Even if your conversation doesn't end in immediate resolution, it should at least serve as a warning to your colleague that you're aware of what he's doing and you're not afraid to confront him. His behavior isn't scaring you away. He's far less likely to be abusive to you if he knows he'll have to look you in the eye once a week at a project check-in.

When Your Colleague Is More Than a Jerk

Working through your challenges with someone you really don't like is important, says Dattner. But that's not the same thing as working through an issue with someone you don't trust. If you doubt someone's integrity, intentions, and ethics, it's time for a more formal approach. If you feel that her behavior crosses the line from annoying to offensive and your personal conversations have not been fruitful, make a case to your boss that the person is destructive to the organization. This is for behavior beyond interrupting colleagues in meetings. Someone who consistently takes credit for work she didn't do, fudges expenses, or never completes her part of projects on time may merit your documenting offenses before that conversation with your boss. You don't necessarily have to "out" your colleague in the first conversation with a boss or HR, says Dattner. You might start by saying, "I think it would be really helpful if you could review the hostile work environment policy with our entire group." Your boss will pick up that something is off, but you haven't pulled a fire alarm yet.

If you witness your colleague berating someone else or pick up on ill will in a meeting, other people may be struggling with that person, too. Work together to keep detailed notes of your colleague's offensive behavior, and go as a group to complain to your manager. "That's the long game," Sutton says. Such a backstage political mobilization takes time, patience, and a good eye for what offenses actually merit complaining to the boss—but it can be effective. For example, Sutton recalls the story of a government worker who faced a nasty and racist coworker. But her complaints to her boss fell on deaf ears. So she gathered some coworkers who also found the woman's actions offensive, and together they assembled what they called "the Asshole Diaries," where they recorded the woman's behavior for a month. With the documentation and support of her peers, the woman was able to present her concerns to her boss more formally. "The woman was gone in two days," Sutton says.

Zen Out

Sometimes we all have to learn what Sutton calls "the fine art of emotional detachment." You don't have to *like* someone who rubs you the wrong way, but you don't have to go insane over it, either. Ask yourself, A year from now, will this still be important to me? If it's something that you can probably let run off your back this week and it will be forgotten the next, then that's what you should do. Don't decide that every annoyance is DEFCON 1. Let some of them go. When brokering a compromise between warring teammates, one manager used to tell her people, "You can only object to two things here. Decide which those two issues are. The rest you just have to live with." It forced her team to isolate what mattered most to them. And that focus helped them find a way to navigate the dispute. The same tactic could help you decide which, if any, battles to pick with your colleague.

Although the daily squabbles can wear on you, keep the long-term view in mind. You never know when your paths will cross with someone's again. "Years after I stopped working with this guy I couldn't stand, I got a reference call for him out of the blue. He was applying for a job with someone I had worked for at a different company," recalls Gary, a senior manager in an investment bank. "It was kind of the revenge moment handed to me on a silver platter." He'd daydreamed of this opportunity in the years they'd worked together. So what did Gary do? "I told the guy who called me that I'd call him back. I thought about what I'd say for a long time. In the end, I gave him a fair review. I said I hadn't enjoyed working with him, but I knew lots of people who did. It was hard, but I decided a slamming review would reflect worse on me than the guy. I actually felt better about myself after that."

That, says Dattner, was the right thing to do. "Don't write anybody off. Don't succumb to negativity. Try to stay positive. Shifting alliances and relationships are what make human life interesting."

Chapter 16
Forging Alliances

The company you keep professionally has a big impact on how you're judged, how much you know about what's going on in your industry and organization, and how effective you can be in executing strategy and initiatives. You want professional relationships that will reflect well on you and will provide you with camaraderie, support, and opportunities.

You're already actively networking; isn't that enough? Real alliances go a step beyond trading favors. More than maintaining a career contact or finding a lunch buddy, making an alliance is a deliberate choice to find and nurture professional relationships with people you like, respect, and want to work beside. When you forge such partnerships, your allies will support your point of view, ask you to work with them on interesting projects, and, essentially, pick you for their team when they can. You've seen alliances at work in politics (consider the "special friendship" between the United States and the United Kingdom in times of world conflict) and in boardroom battles—and even in reality television, where powerful alliances can eject or keep particular players in the game. But because alliances can be so powerful (see chapter 8, "The Clique"), you must proceed with caution in building and maintaining the right set of relationships for your career—and disengaging from them when the time is right. Here's what the experts have to say.

How to Form Alliances

Ideally, you'll build alliances based on supportive behavior, a perceived sense of shared values, and loyalty. "Alliances are really a sense of having a collective identity," observes communication and branding expert Dorie Clark. "We think of ourselves as a team that advances all its members." Most alliances start informally, but that's not to say you shouldn't proactively look for opportunities to form or build on natural affinity. For example, you might speak up in a meeting to back your colleague's idea. Several weeks later, she may offer to help with your project even though she wasn't formally assigned to it. You begin making a point of stopping by her desk to catch up on the redesign effort she's leading—and soon you become engaged and interested in keeping up. Often alliances are that obvious and natural. You like—and are like—certain colleagues, and you want to work with them and be around them. You develop true work friendships.

Other times you deliberately and strategically form alliances to fulfill a need. For example, if your company's hottest area of growth and development is outside your area of expertise, you might look for opportunities to form alliances with people in that group who are involved in interesting projects as a way of orienting yourself with the work they're doing. Or perhaps you're the one in the hottest area of the company, but your work is so cutting edge that people don't understand it and therefore aren't inclined to support it. That's when you need people in your court. "Innovators cannot work in isolation if they want their concepts to catch on," explains Harvard Business School professor Rosabeth Moss Kanter in her classic *Harvard Business Review* article "Innovation: The Classic Traps." Those innovators "must build coalitions of supporters who will provide air cover for the project, speak up for them in meetings they don't attend, or sponsor the embryonic innovation as it moves into the next stages of diffusion and use."

Meeting these kinds of specific needs calls for proactive alliance building on your part. Suppose you're shy on technology skills; you might look for someone in the tech group who could answer your questions, offer guidance, and suggest ways to keep up with advancing technology more easily. Set up a monthly lunch group with peers whom you consider high potential to informally network and discuss what's going on in the company. Volunteer to grab a sandwich for Marisol in finance at month end when you're running out for yourself. She'll likely return the favor by making sure your vendors are paid on time. You don't want to be phony or inauthentic, but building a genuine alliance requires getting to know and respect each other well enough that you're in frequent contact and you're willing to ask for—and return—favors.

To do this strategically, you must identify the right people to build connections with, ways to take your relationships beyond good will and intentions, and means to keep your alliances healthy and productive. Let's look at each step.

Pick the right people

Bosses are often natural allies, helping their direct reports quickly advance through the ranks. Whitney Johnson, author of *Dare, Dream, Do,* benefited from hitching her wagon to a high-achieving boss early in her career. "In that instance, having an alliance was a very good thing," Johnson remembers. "I was considered part of his inner circle—and he took me through three different career moves with him."

But a strong set of alliances should go up, down, and sideways across the organization, she advises. So consider alliances with people who are lower down in the organizational hierarchy—key gatekeepers to information and power, such as your boss's assistant or the person who staffs the tech help desk. Acknowledging the contributions of people who are often overlooked and making a connection with them can support their work—and yours. It could be as simple as passing along a sincere compliment on a tech's work to the support desk director. When it comes time for your department's software updates, you just might find that your IT ally schedules your group's work for a time that's actually convenient for them because of the connection you've made.

Your alliances are like your investment portfolio. You wouldn't put all your assets into one hot stock; you'd sensibly spread them out to ensure that you ride out any bumps in the economy. That same approach applies to your connections. Balance your relationships, forming unexpected and surprising alliances when possible, Clark says. "You don't want to be permanently pigeonholed. Make sure you're perceived as distinct from what may be seen as your natural group." For example, people might assume that all under-30s in the company gravitate toward each other because they're in the same generation. Make an effort to connect instead with people who come from various backgrounds, reflect different demographics, or have dissimilar skills from yours. Reaching out to people who aren't like you will strengthen your personal network and also expand your worldview and potential for diverse thinking, according to research from leadership and networking expert Brian Uzzi. And as with a stock investment, you shouldn't count on each alliance to pay immediate dividends. Some relationships develop and extend over many years. You never know where and when someone will be critical to your career.

If you're new to an organization, proceed slowly. You have to first figure out the political landscape before you choose allies so that you're certain they're well respected and have the potential to help you in your career. "You never want to align yourself too rapidly to any faction," cautions Clark. "If you're operating in a polarizing work environment—and you don't know it—you might find that you've unintentionally aligned yourself with the

Montagues or the Capulets." Be pleasant to everyone until you know the lay of the land.

Once you've identified the right people, how can you build, maintain, and deepen your relationships?

Be a good ally

You can start by looking for ways to connect with someone you think can help you advance your career. Be a go-to person for her. Volunteer to help with projects. Enthusiastically participate in programs, outings, or working lunches she organizes. Be engaged. Find opportunities to support her behind the scenes and make her look good in front of her peers or her boss.

Alliances, like friendships, need tending to stay healthy. You can't simply back someone a few times and then expect the relationship to be strong months and years down the line. Regular contact with your allies (from serendipitous run-ins to scheduled lunch dates) helps you stay in sync. And an important part of having a good ally is to *be* a good ally. How do you do that? "Effective communication forms the foundation for a positive work alliance," says organizational development and HR expert Susan Heathfield. "You need to tell your potential ally what you need and listen deeply to what she needs. Open lines of communication keep information, opinions, and support flowing." Support your colleague's goals. Give her credit when it's due. Be an early endorser; if you support your colleague's ideas and work, then speak up and say so before you see which direction the rest of the group is heading.

On the other hand, don't be afraid to be an honest sounding board. When you think your ally is making a mistake or his position isn't right, say so—in private. "You can say 'George, as much as I like you and generally support your point of view, in this instance I'm in complete disagreement and won't be able to publicly support that direction,'" Heathfield says. Reassure him that this has nothing to do with your long-term support for him but is only a single area of disagreement. And emphasize that in fact it's probably a good thing that the two of you are seen to disagree from time to time. It establishes that you're not always simply singing in unison but rather bringing two distinct sets of skills and opinions to your workplace.

To keep your relationship with your current allies strong and continually grow new ones, you have to find ways to stay in regular contact. Ask whether you can occasionally attend standing meetings led by your ally as a way to keep up to speed with her department's issues. Add private calendar reminders to check in with people routinely or before or after something important you know is happening for them: "How did that presentation go?" or "Would you like to do a practice run with me before you meet with the department heads?"

Being a good ally, then, means looking for ways to involve yourself and support the work and growth of your colleague. If you want her to be interested in helping you, you need to be genuinely interested in helping her.

Know when to cut ties

Your pool of allies needs not only frequent tending but also regular assessment. And sometimes your review will indicate that it's time to rethink who's in your cabinet.

What happens when your ally begins acting in ways that you don't admire? Or when getting to know the person yields unflattering information? When an ally does questionable things, your career—and your reputation—can come into question, too. Dmitry, now a consultant and author, recalls the heady thrill of being singled out as an ally of a rising, powerful investment banker early in his career. But even though his boss provided him with wonderful career opportunities, he came to see that she also used him to push around other staff who got in her way. For example, she would convince him that certain people were problems in the workplace, so Dmitry would then complain to other peers and superiors about her targets—and in one case his words helped push someone out of a job. Once the junior banker realized how destructive his ally was, he looked for opportunities to get out of that work group. It was, in hindsight, an important lesson. "You're looking for that experience like high school or a college fraternity where you *belong*," he says now. "But that fraternity comes with a price."

If your ally has done something you find distasteful or problematic, others' perception of your colleague's actions will reflect on you, too. People might assume that because you're so closely aligned you'll defend his mistakes and bad attitude. If a close association falls from grace, you could also find yourself tarnished. And when an ally leaves, your boss and peers may assume that you'll follow. If your ally fails to get a promotion, others may assume that your allegiance is so strong that you won't work with the person who was chosen instead.

When you find yourself faced with one of these scenarios, you have the opportunity to proactively manage people's perceptions of you and the situation. In the case of the ally who misses out on a promotion, for example, don't give anyone time to think you'll give the new person guff on your ally's behalf. Immediately go see the person who got the job, advises Heathfield, and make clear that you're looking forward to working with her and will support her in her new position. Act early, and control the message rather than leave it open to speculation and misinterpretation.

Even if your ally doesn't make a catastrophic mistake, most alliances won't be useful forever. "Don't align yourself too strongly or too permanently with anyone," suggests Johnson. It's like a Hollywood model of moviemaking: Gather the best people around you to make something great. But when filming wraps, and the movie has been promoted and had its run, you can and should look for other groups to work with. It's beneficial to review and refresh—or prune—your alliances. Keep any that have immediate or foreseeable benefits for you, and let others fade. "Either politely distance yourself," Johnson advises, or find respectful ways to just do less and less work together.

Decades ago, when Susan Heathfield was first hired in a human resources position at General Motors, she knew she had been dropped into the deep end of the pool. Her previous experience had been in education, so entering the siloed world of union/management politics required finesse. But she quickly identified a key union line manager. "I went directly to him and said, 'Ron, I'm completely out of my element. I want to add value, but I can't do it without knowing more than I do.'" Ron introduced her to skilled tradespeople and immersed her in the life of the plant in a way that earned her respect from the union workers, who otherwise might have been wary of her intentions. "He had the tool and die guys invite me to their meetings. And then each group invited me." Little by little, Heathfield earned not only Ron's respect but also the respect of all the union workers in the plant. She was eventually invited to attend *both* union and management strategy sessions in advance of difficult negotiations.

And Ron benefited from their alliance, too. "I always put him forth as someone to be depended on, someone to be consulted," Heathfield says. "I learned so much from Ron about creating relationships and adding value." When you're thoughtful about picking and maintaining the right set of allies, the relationships can pay dividends for years—for both of you.

Index

Index

Index

About the Author

Karen Dillon is a coauthor of the *New York Times* best-seller *How Will You Measure Your Life?* (with Clayton M. Christensen and James Allworth). She is the former editor of *Harvard Business Review* and is now a contributing editor. She's also Global Ambassador to The Legal 500. A graduate of Cornell University and Northwestern University's Medill School of Journalism, Dillon began managing people very early in her career, which led to a particular interest in the topics of leadership, developing talent, and managing yourself. Ashoka, a global network of social entrepreneurs, named her one of the world's most influential and inspiring women in 2011. Follow her on Twitter @DillonHBR.

Notes

Notes

Notes

Notes

Notes

Notes

Notes

Notes

Notes

Notes

Notes

Notes

Notes

Notes

Notes

Notes

Smart advice and inspiration from a source you trust.

Harvard Business Review Guides

Packed with concise, practical tips from leading experts—and examples that make them easy to apply—the HBR Guides series provides smart answers to your most pressing work challenges. Arm yourself with the advice you need to succeed on the job, from the most trusted brand in business.

**AVAILABLE IN PAPERBACK
OR EBOOK FORMAT
WHEREVER BOOKS ARE SOLD**

- Better Business Writing
- Coaching Employees
- Finance Basics for Managers
- Getting the Mentoring You Need
- Getting the Right Work Done

- Managing Stress at Work
- Managing Up and Across
- Office Politics
- Persuasive Presentations
- Project Management

BUY FOR YOUR TEAM, COMPANY, OR EVENT.
To learn more about bulk discounts visit hbr.org.